AF510009

Protector Paradigms

Supporting inmate journeys towards responsible community re-entry

Alaric Thomas

Table of Contents

1 Chapter 1: Understanding the Re-entry Landscape

Re-entering society after incarceration is not simply a matter of walking out the prison gates. It's a complex, multifaceted journey fraught with challenges that can feel overwhelming to the individual and require a comprehensive understanding from those who seek to support them. The societal landscape into which formerly incarcerated individuals return has profound impact. It is shaped by interconnected factors like economic realities, housing availability, employment opportunities, and prevailing public perceptions.

A significant barrier lies in the immediate post-release period. The individual often lacks basic necessities: stable housing, adequate food, and appropriate clothing. This vulnerability can quickly lead to desperation, making it difficult to focus on long-term goals such as finding employment or engaging in rehabilitation programs. Finding affordable housing is a colossal challenge. Many landlords are hesitant to rent to individuals with criminal records, further limiting options and potentially pushing people into homelessness, especially those that come out from Probation services.

Employment is another critical hurdle. Many employers are reluctant to hire individuals with a criminal background, even for entry-level positions. This reluctance is often fueled by fear and misconceptions about the risk of recidivism. Even when employment is secured, maintaining it can be difficult due to lack of skills, experience, or simply the inability to adjust to workplace demands after prolonged incarceration. Industrial or vocational training is a fundamental part of the re-entry process. Without it, the individual may be unable to find a job to sustain their life.

Beyond the practical barriers, the psychological and social challenges can be equally daunting. Stigma and discrimination are pervasive, creating a sense of isolation and hindering successful reintegration. Formerly incarcerated individuals may face rejection from family and friends, making it difficult to rebuild supportive relationships. This can lead to feelings of shame, hopelessness, and a heightened risk of relapse into criminal behavior. Mental health issues, often exacerbated by the experience of incarceration, can further complicate the re-entry process. Trauma, anxiety, and depression are common among formerly incarcerated individuals and can significantly impact their ability to cope with the challenges of re-entry, requiring access to adequate Mental health services.

Community support plays a vital role in mitigating these challenges. This support can take many forms, from providing transitional housing and job training to offering mental health counseling and peer support groups. Community organizations, faith-based groups, and individual volunteers can all contribute to creating a welcoming and supportive environment for formerly incarcerated individuals. Furthermore, a strong support network can provide a sense of belonging and purpose, helping individuals to overcome feelings of isolation and hopelessness. Victimology and victims of crime are an important consideration for re-entry. The awareness of crime and the damage it causes is an important factor to take into account.

Responsible re-entry goes beyond simply avoiding re-arrest. It encompasses a broader commitment to personal growth, community engagement, and making amends for past harm. It means taking responsibility for one's actions, developing healthy coping mechanisms, and contributing positively to society. It also involves acknowledging the impact of one's crime on victims and working to repair the harm caused. Responsible re-entry is not a passive process; it requires active participation and a willingness to learn and grow. It's a commitment to becoming a productive and law-abiding member of the community, and it's a journey that requires ongoing support and encouragement. Ultimately, responsible re-entry is about creating a safer and more just society for all.

1.1 Barriers to Successful Re-entry

One of the most formidable barriers faced upon release is simply securing stable housing. Without a safe and reliable place to live, individuals struggle to find employment, maintain sobriety, and attend required meetings with parole officers or treatment providers. Landlords are often hesitant to rent to individuals with criminal records, fearing property damage or disruption to other tenants. This hesitancy is compounded by a national shortage of affordable housing, which puts formerly incarcerated individuals at a distinct disadvantage compared to other renters. Some cities have implemented "fair chance" housing policies, which prevent landlords from automatically denying housing based solely on a criminal record, but these policies are not yet widespread and often contain loopholes. Emergency shelters exist, but they are often overcrowded, lack privacy, and may not be conducive to long-term recovery. Transitional housing programs can offer a temporary solution, providing a structured environment with support services, but these programs often have long waiting lists and limited capacity. Finding a place to call home isn't just a matter of comfort; it's a foundation for rebuilding a life.

Beyond the immediate need for shelter, the challenges of finding meaningful employment represent another significant hurdle. Many formerly incarcerated individuals lack the education, skills, and work experience needed to compete in today's job market. Even those with marketable skills often face discrimination from employers who are reluctant to hire someone with a criminal record. Background checks are commonplace, and a conviction can be a permanent stain on an applicant's record, regardless of the nature of the offense or the length of time that has passed since release. Some employers are willing to "ban the box," removing the question about criminal history from the initial application, but the issue often resurfaces later in the hiring process. Furthermore, certain professions are automatically off-limits to individuals with specific types of convictions, regardless of their qualifications. This combination of limited skills, employer bias, and legal restrictions makes finding a job a daunting task, leading to frustration, discouragement, and an increased risk of recidivism. I recall the story of Michael, who completed a welding program while incarcerated and earned several certifications. Despite his qualifications, he was repeatedly turned down for welding jobs because of a past drug conviction. He eventually found work as a day laborer, far below his skill level, which only deepened his sense of hopelessness.

Adding another layer of complexity, the erosion of social support networks during incarceration can be devastating. Maintaining relationships with family and friends becomes difficult due to geographical distance, limited communication opportunities, and the stigma associated with imprisonment. Upon release, individuals may find that their relationships have deteriorated or dissolved altogether. Family members may be unwilling or unable to provide support, either because they lack the resources or because they have been hurt by the individual's past actions. The absence of a supportive social network can lead to feelings of isolation, loneliness, and depression, making it even harder to navigate the challenges of re-entry. Finding new, healthy social connections can be difficult, especially for individuals who are struggling with substance abuse or mental health issues. Support groups and faith-based organizations can provide a sense of community and belonging, but it takes time and effort to build trust and establish meaningful relationships.

The weight of financial burdens also crushes many returning citizens. Fines, court costs, restitution payments, and child support arrears can accumulate during incarceration, creating a significant debt burden upon release. Finding a job that pays enough to cover these expenses, along with basic living expenses, can be nearly impossible. Many individuals are forced to rely on public assistance, which is often inadequate to meet their needs. The pressure to earn money can lead some to engage in illegal activities, further increasing their risk of re-incarceration. Additionally, access to financial services, such as bank accounts and credit cards, can be limited due to their criminal history. This makes it difficult to manage their finances and build a positive credit history. Simple tasks, such as renting an apartment or buying a car, become much more challenging when they are unable to demonstrate financial responsibility.

Finally, it is also important to recognize that the stigma associated with incarceration can be a significant barrier to successful re-entry. Formerly incarcerated individuals often face discrimination and prejudice in all aspects of their lives, from housing and employment to education and social interactions. They may be labeled as "criminals" or "felons" and treated with suspicion and distrust. This stigma can lead to feelings of shame, guilt, and self-doubt, making it harder to build a positive self-image and pursue their goals. Overcoming stigma requires not only individual resilience but also systemic change. Educating the public about the challenges of re-entry and promoting understanding and empathy can help to reduce prejudice and create a more welcoming environment for formerly incarcerated individuals. Changing laws and policies that perpetuate discrimination, such as restrictions on voting rights and occupational licensing, is also essential. It requires a concerted effort from individuals, organizations, and policymakers to create a society that embraces second chances and supports successful re-entry.

1.2 The Role of Community Support

The journey from incarceration back into society is rarely a solitary one, and the strength of the network surrounding a returning citizen significantly impacts their chances of success. I've seen firsthand how a supportive community can be the difference between a revolving door and a fresh start. But what exactly constitutes "community support," and how can we cultivate it effectively? It's more than just offering a handout; it's about building bridges, fostering understanding, and providing the resources and relationships needed to thrive. Effective community support goes beyond simply providing material assistance. I remember a man, let's call him David, who was released after serving fifteen years. He had a place to stay at a halfway house, but he felt isolated and overwhelmed. The halfway house offered shelter, but it wasn't a community. What truly helped him was finding a local church group that welcomed him, not as a former inmate, but as a human being. They provided him with meals, helped him with job applications, and, most importantly, offered him a sense of belonging. This highlights the critical role of social inclusion in the re-entry process. It's about creating spaces where returning citizens feel valued, respected, and understood. Churches, community centers, and even online forums can serve as vital platforms for connection and support. The key is to foster genuine relationships built on empathy and mutual respect.

Access to practical resources is, of course, undeniable. One of the biggest hurdles returning citizens face is finding safe and affordable housing. Without a stable place to live, it's incredibly difficult to secure employment, maintain sobriety, or rebuild family relationships. Shelters, transitional housing programs, and assistance with finding permanent housing are essential components of community support. Similarly, access to employment opportunities is crucial for financial stability and self-sufficiency. Job training programs, resume writing workshops, and connections to local employers can make a significant difference. It's also important to consider the specific needs of each individual. Some returning citizens may require assistance with transportation, childcare, or healthcare. Connecting them with relevant community services can help them overcome these barriers and focus on their re-entry goals. Providing assistance is about more than just meeting basic needs; it's about empowering individuals to take control of their lives.

The community also plays a vital role in advocating for policy changes that support successful re-entry. Many laws and policies create unnecessary barriers for returning citizens, such as restrictions on housing, employment, and voting rights. By advocating for fairer policies, communities can help level the playing field and create more opportunities for successful re-entry. Educating the public about the challenges returning citizens face is also essential. Many people hold negative stereotypes and misconceptions about formerly incarcerated individuals, which can lead to discrimination and social exclusion. By sharing accurate information and personal stories, we can challenge these stereotypes and promote understanding and empathy. This will allow all of society to embrace the returning citizens and provide them with the resources they desperately need.

However, community support isn't without its challenges. Funding limitations, lack of coordination among service providers, and community resistance can all hinder efforts to support returning citizens. To address these challenges, it's important to build strong partnerships between government agencies, non-profit organizations, and community members. Collaboration and communication are essential for ensuring that resources are used effectively and that returning citizens receive the comprehensive support they need. Building trust within the community is also crucial. Some residents may be hesitant to support returning citizens, fearing that they will pose a threat to public safety. By demonstrating a commitment to accountability and transparency, organizations can build trust and overcome resistance. After all, the best community support happens when the community feels safe.

Consider this: In my work, I've found that mentoring programs can be incredibly effective in supporting returning citizens. Connecting individuals with positive role models who can provide guidance, support, and encouragement can make a significant difference in their re-entry journey. Mentors can help returning citizens navigate the challenges of finding employment, building healthy relationships, and avoiding relapse. They can also provide a sense of hope and possibility, reminding individuals that they are not alone and that they are capable of achieving their goals. The connection with another person can be all the change and hope they need.

Ultimately, the role of community support is to create a welcoming and inclusive environment where returning citizens can rebuild their lives and become productive members of society. It's about recognizing their humanity, valuing their potential, and providing them with the resources and relationships they need to succeed. It's about understanding that re-entry is not just an individual journey, but a community responsibility. Every step of the way needs support from the community around them. By working together, we can create a more just and equitable society where everyone has the opportunity to thrive. It takes a village to raise a child, and in many ways, it takes a community to help a person re-enter society successfully.

So, how can you contribute? Volunteer your time, donate to local organizations, advocate for policy changes, or simply reach out to a returning citizen and offer your support. Every act of kindness, no matter how small, can make a difference in someone's life.

1.3 Defining Responsible Re-entry

Responsible re-entry, at its core, is more than just staying out of prison. It's about becoming a contributing member of society, a process that demands a multifaceted approach encompassing personal responsibility, community support, and a willingness to embrace positive change. Defining this concept with clarity is crucial because it shapes the expectations and goals of everyone involved – the individual re-entering, their family, the community, and the correctional system itself. It's a holistic transformation, an evolution from a life often marked by adversity and perhaps poor choices, to one characterized by stability, purpose, and contribution. I think of it as a phoenix rising, but this phoenix needs nurturing and guidance.

The traditional definition of successful re-entry, often measured solely by recidivism rates, falls short. While avoiding re-incarceration is undoubtedly a vital indicator, it doesn't capture the full spectrum of positive outcomes that are possible. A person might technically stay out of prison, but still struggle with unemployment, homelessness, addiction, or mental health issues. Are they truly thriving? Are they fulfilling their potential? Are they making a positive impact on their community? A truly responsible re-entry encompasses these broader aspects of well-being and social integration. It considers the individual's overall quality of life, their relationships, their contributions to the community, and their sense of purpose. We need to move beyond simply avoiding negative outcomes and focus on fostering positive ones.

Economic self-sufficiency is a cornerstone of responsible re-entry. Securing stable employment not only provides financial independence but also fosters a sense of dignity and self-worth. This means having marketable skills, a realistic career plan, and the resources to navigate the job market effectively. It includes addressing any educational deficits, providing vocational training, and offering support with job searching, resume writing, and interview skills. But it also means removing barriers to employment, such as discriminatory hiring practices, and creating opportunities for individuals with criminal records to prove themselves. Employers need to be willing to give people a second chance, and society needs to challenge the stigma that often prevents them from doing so. Moreover, financial literacy is key; understanding budgeting, saving, and managing debt empowers individuals to maintain their financial stability long-term.

Beyond economic factors, responsible re-entry necessitates addressing mental health and substance abuse issues. Many individuals entering society have a history of trauma, mental illness, or addiction. These issues can significantly impede their ability to reintegrate successfully if left untreated. Providing access to mental health services, substance abuse treatment programs, and support groups is essential. This includes not only individual therapy but also group counseling, peer support, and medication management. A trauma-informed approach is crucial, recognizing the impact of past experiences on current behavior and tailoring treatment accordingly. Building resilience, developing coping mechanisms, and fostering a sense of hope are all vital components of this process. After all, a sound mind is often required for one to remain at peace, and avoid conflicts.

Furthermore, a strong support system is critical for successful re-entry. Rebuilding relationships with family and friends can provide a sense of belonging and emotional support. However, it's important to acknowledge that some relationships may be unhealthy or even harmful. In such cases, it may be necessary to establish new, positive connections with individuals who can provide encouragement and guidance. Community-based organizations, faith-based groups, and mentoring programs can play a vital role in providing this support. These organizations can offer practical assistance with housing, transportation, and other essential needs, as well as emotional support and guidance. Connecting individuals with these resources and fostering a sense of community can significantly increase their chances of success.

Legal and ethical considerations are also paramount. Individuals entering society must understand their legal obligations, including parole or probation requirements, and comply with all applicable laws. This includes avoiding criminal behavior, maintaining contact with their parole officer, and adhering to any restrictions on their movements or activities. Ethical decision-making is also essential. It means making choices that are consistent with one's values and that do not harm oneself or others. Victim awareness programs can help individuals understand the impact of their crimes on victims and develop empathy and remorse. Restorative justice principles can provide an opportunity for individuals to make amends for their past actions and contribute to the healing process. The goal is not only to avoid re-offending but also to repair the harm caused by their crimes and contribute to a safer, more just society.

Finally, responsible re-entry is a continuous process, not a one-time event. It requires ongoing support, encouragement, and accountability. Individuals entering society will inevitably face challenges and setbacks. It's important to have strategies in place for dealing with these challenges and to have access to resources that can provide assistance when needed. This might include relapse prevention plans, crisis intervention services, or ongoing counseling. It also means fostering a culture of forgiveness and second chances, where individuals are given the opportunity to learn from their mistakes and move forward in a positive direction. Ultimately, responsible re-entry is a shared responsibility, requiring the commitment of individuals, families, communities, and the correctional system. By working together, we can create a system that supports successful re-entry, reduces recidivism, and promotes safer, more just communities for all.

2 Chapter 2: Trauma-Informed Approaches

Trauma's pervasive impact often remains hidden beneath the surface of an inmate's behavior. It isn't merely a past event; it's a deeply ingrained experience that reshapes their cognitive, emotional, and behavioral responses. Understanding this profound impact is the cornerstone of any effective re-entry program. Before we can assist individuals in building a better future, we must acknowledge and address the wounds they carry from their past. Many have endured adverse childhood experiences (ACEs), witnessing or experiencing violence, neglect, or abuse. These experiences can lead to chronic stress, difficulty regulating emotions, impaired decision-making, and a heightened sensitivity to perceived threats. In essence, their brains and bodies are constantly on high alert, interpreting situations through the lens of past trauma. This hypervigilance can manifest as irritability, anger outbursts, difficulty concentrating, and a tendency to withdraw from social interactions. It's crucial to remember that these are not simply character flaws or willful defiance; they are often survival mechanisms developed in response to overwhelming adversity. Ignoring this history is not only insensitive but also undermines the effectiveness of any intervention. A trauma-informed approach requires us to shift our perspective, moving away from asking, "What's wrong with this person?" to asking, "What happened to this person?" This fundamental shift in mindset allows us to approach inmates with empathy, compassion, and a deeper understanding of their underlying needs.

Building trust with individuals who have experienced trauma is an essential, yet often challenging, aspect of the re-entry process. Past experiences of betrayal, abuse, or neglect can make them hesitant to form new relationships or to trust authority figures. To overcome this barrier, we must consistently demonstrate trustworthiness through our actions and words. This involves being reliable, honest, and transparent in our interactions. Keep your promises, follow through on commitments, and be upfront about the limitations of your role. Avoid making false promises or exaggerating the resources available to them. Consistency is key. Inconsistent behavior, even if unintentional, can trigger past traumas and reinforce their distrust. It's also important to be mindful of your body language and tone of voice. A non-judgmental and empathetic approach can create a sense of safety and security. Active listening is crucial. Give inmates the opportunity to share their stories without interruption or judgment. Validate their feelings and acknowledge the difficulties they have faced. Resist the urge to offer unsolicited advice or to minimize their experiences. Simply listening and bearing witness to their pain can be incredibly healing. Furthermore, creating a predictable and structured environment can also foster trust. Clear expectations, consistent routines, and transparent communication can help to reduce anxiety and create a sense of stability. Provide inmates with clear information about the re-entry process, their rights and responsibilities, and the resources available to them. Uncertainty and ambiguity can be particularly triggering for individuals who have experienced trauma, so clarity and consistency are essential. It's important to recognize that building trust is an ongoing process, not a one-time event. It requires patience, persistence, and a genuine commitment to creating a safe and supportive environment.

Safety, both physical and emotional, is paramount in facilitating healing and promoting successful re-entry. Individuals who have experienced trauma often feel unsafe in the world, constantly anticipating danger and bracing themselves for the worst. Creating a sense of safety involves more than just providing a secure physical environment. It also requires addressing the emotional and psychological needs of inmates. This begins with establishing clear boundaries and enforcing rules consistently and fairly. Predictability and structure can help to create a sense of stability and reduce anxiety. It's also important to be mindful of the language and communication styles used within the correctional facility. Avoid using harsh or demeaning language, and promote a culture of respect and empathy. Encourage positive interactions between inmates and staff, and provide opportunities for them to build supportive relationships. Creating a safe environment also involves addressing issues of power and control. Individuals who have experienced trauma often feel powerless and vulnerable, so it's important to empower them to make choices and to take control of their lives. Provide them with opportunities to participate in decision-making processes, and respect their autonomy and independence. Additionally, it's crucial to be aware of potential triggers that may evoke past traumas. Loud noises, sudden movements, or certain smells can all trigger traumatic memories and lead to emotional distress. Create a calm and predictable environment, and provide inmates with coping strategies for managing triggers. This might involve teaching them relaxation techniques, mindfulness exercises, or grounding techniques. Moreover, it's essential to provide access to mental health services for inmates who have experienced trauma. Therapy, counseling, and support groups can provide them with a safe space to process their experiences, develop coping skills, and heal from their wounds. A trauma-informed approach recognizes that safety is not just the absence of danger, but also the presence of connection, support, and empowerment. By creating a safe and supportive environment, we can help inmates to heal from their past traumas and build a brighter future.

2.1 Recognizing Trauma's Impact

Trauma leaves an indelible mark, etching itself onto the lives of those who experience it. Often, this impact is subtle, manifesting in ways that might not be immediately recognized, particularly within the inmate population. We, as those aiming to support their re-entry, must develop a keen eye for identifying these signs, as they are often the key to unlocking healing and progress.

The effects of trauma are diverse and far-reaching, influencing nearly every aspect of an individual's life. For a person who has lived through abuse, violence, or neglect, particularly during childhood, the world can feel like a fundamentally unsafe place. This sense of insecurity can manifest in a variety of ways, from hypervigilance and anxiety to difficulty forming trusting relationships. I've seen it time and again – the guarded posture, the averted gaze, the reluctance to share personal information. These are not necessarily signs of defiance or resistance, but often symptoms of a deeply ingrained fear of vulnerability. Furthermore, trauma can significantly impair cognitive function, affecting memory, concentration, and decision-making abilities. This can create significant challenges for inmates attempting to participate in educational programs, vocational training, or even simple daily routines. It's crucial to remember that these cognitive difficulties are not indicative of a lack of intelligence or motivation, but rather a consequence of the brain's response to overwhelming stress.

One of the most common manifestations of trauma is emotional dysregulation. This can present as intense mood swings, irritability, anger outbursts, or even emotional numbness. Individuals struggling with emotional dysregulation may find it difficult to manage their impulses, leading to behavioral problems and difficulties in interpersonal relationships. They might react disproportionately to seemingly minor stressors, or they might withdraw and isolate themselves from others. Recognizing that these emotional and behavioral patterns are often rooted in past trauma is essential for developing effective support strategies. Instead of reacting with judgment or punishment, we must respond with empathy and understanding, providing inmates with the tools and resources they need to regulate their emotions and develop healthier coping mechanisms. This might involve individual therapy, group counseling, or mindfulness-based practices.

The impact of trauma extends beyond individual functioning, profoundly affecting interpersonal relationships. Individuals with a history of trauma may struggle to form and maintain healthy relationships, often experiencing difficulty with trust, intimacy, and communication. They might be prone to repeating unhealthy relationship patterns, such as seeking out partners who are abusive or neglectful, or they might isolate themselves from others altogether, fearing further rejection or harm. It's important to acknowledge that these relational difficulties are not a reflection of a person's character or worth, but rather a consequence of their past experiences. I believe that by providing inmates with opportunities to develop healthy relationship skills, such as communication, empathy, and boundary setting, we can help them break free from these destructive patterns and build more fulfilling connections with others.

Another crucial aspect of recognizing trauma's impact is understanding the potential for re-traumatization. This occurs when an individual is exposed to situations, environments, or interactions that trigger memories or feelings associated with their past trauma. For incarcerated individuals, the prison environment itself can be inherently re-traumatizing, with its inherent power dynamics, lack of control, and potential for violence. Even seemingly innocuous situations, such as being subjected to loud noises or confined spaces, can trigger flashbacks or panic attacks. Therefore, it is imperative that correctional staff and re-entry support providers are trained to recognize and prevent re-traumatization. This involves creating a safe and predictable environment, avoiding the use of punitive or coercive measures, and providing inmates with opportunities to exercise control and autonomy whenever possible. By minimizing the risk of re-traumatization, we can create a more conducive environment for healing and growth.

Self-harm and suicidal ideation are also potential indicators of unresolved trauma. When individuals feel overwhelmed by their past experiences, they may turn to self-harm as a way to cope with intense emotional pain. This can manifest in various forms, from cutting and burning to substance abuse and reckless behavior. Suicidal ideation, the contemplation of suicide, is another serious consequence of trauma. Individuals who feel hopeless and overwhelmed by their past may see suicide as the only way to escape their pain. Recognizing these warning signs and providing immediate access to mental health services is crucial for preventing tragic outcomes. This requires a collaborative effort between correctional staff, mental health professionals, and re-entry support providers, all working together to

ensure that inmates receive the care and support they need.
Finally, it is important to acknowledge that trauma can manifest differently in different individuals. There is no one-size-fits-all approach to recognizing or addressing its impact. Some individuals may be outwardly expressive of their pain, while others may be more withdrawn and guarded. Some may exhibit clear symptoms of post-traumatic stress disorder (PTSD), while others may struggle with more subtle, less easily identifiable issues. Therefore, it is essential to approach each inmate as an individual, taking the time to listen to their story, understand their unique experiences, and tailor our support accordingly. This requires a commitment to empathy, compassion, and cultural sensitivity, as well as a willingness to challenge our own assumptions and biases. By adopting a trauma-informed approach, we can create a more supportive and healing environment for incarcerated individuals, empowering them to overcome their past and build a brighter future. I have found that the key to a successful re-entry often lies in the early recognition and appropriate response to the silent wounds of trauma.

2.2 Building Trust and Safety

Building trust is paramount. It's the bedrock upon which any successful re-entry plan is built. Without it, the strategies and resources offered are likely to fall flat, dismissed as empty promises or, worse, as manipulative tactics. For individuals who have experienced incarceration, trust is often a scarce commodity, eroded by past experiences with the system, with authority figures, and sometimes, even with those closest to them. Therefore, deliberately fostering a climate of trust and safety is not merely a best practice; it's an ethical imperative.

One of the first steps in building this essential trust is consistent and transparent communication. Individuals re-entering society need clear, honest information about what to expect, what is expected of them, and the resources available to them. This means avoiding jargon, speaking plainly, and being upfront about potential challenges and limitations. Hiding information or sugarcoating reality can quickly undermine trust. Instead, embrace radical honesty tempered with empathy and a commitment to support. For instance, if a particular housing program has a long waiting list, be upfront about it. Don't promise immediate placement if it's unrealistic. Instead, offer alternative temporary solutions and guidance on navigating the application process. Similarly, when explaining the conditions of parole or probation, clearly outline the rules and potential consequences of violations, but also emphasize the support available to help them succeed. This transparency demonstrates respect and conveys a genuine desire to see them thrive, not just comply.

Creating a safe environment involves more than just physical security. It means fostering an atmosphere of emotional safety, where individuals feel comfortable expressing their thoughts and feelings without fear of judgment or retribution. Many returning citizens have experienced trauma, abuse, and violence, both inside and outside correctional facilities. These experiences can lead to hypervigilance, anxiety, and difficulty trusting others. As such, actively cultivating a space of non-judgmental acceptance is essential. This can be achieved through active listening, empathetic responses, and a willingness to validate their experiences. Avoid interrupting, offering unsolicited advice, or minimizing their concerns. Instead, focus on truly hearing what they have to say and acknowledging the challenges they face. For example, instead of saying "Just get over it" when someone expresses anger or frustration, acknowledge their feel-

ings by saying, "I understand why you're feeling that way. It sounds like you're dealing with a lot right now." This simple act of validation can go a long way in building trust and fostering a sense of safety.
Furthermore, consistency in actions is key. Words alone are not enough to build trust. Individuals need to see that promises are kept, commitments are honored, and actions align with stated values. This means following through on commitments, being reliable, and demonstrating integrity in all interactions. If you say you will connect someone with a specific resource, make sure you do it. If you promise to follow up on a particular issue, keep your word. Even small acts of inconsistency can erode trust and reinforce negative perceptions. Conversely, consistent and reliable actions build credibility and demonstrate a genuine commitment to their well-being. It shows that you are not just saying the right things, but that you are also willing to put in the effort to support them.
Moreover, empower individuals by giving them choices and control over their re-entry plans. Often, incarcerated individuals have experienced a lack of autonomy and control over their lives. Upon release, it is crucial to empower them to make decisions about their future and to actively participate in shaping their own re-entry journey. This means offering choices, respecting their preferences, and valuing their input. For example, when developing a job search strategy, involve them in identifying their skills, interests, and career goals. Provide them with information about different job options, but ultimately let them decide which path they want to pursue. Similarly, when connecting them with community resources, offer them a range of options and allow them to choose the services that best meet their needs. By empowering individuals to take ownership of their re-entry plans, you not only build trust but also foster a sense of agency and self-efficacy, which are essential for long-term success.

Be aware of your own biases and assumptions. Everyone carries unconscious biases that can influence their perceptions and interactions. It is crucial to be aware of these biases and to actively challenge them in order to avoid perpetuating stereotypes or making assumptions about individuals based on their past. For example, avoid assuming that all formerly incarcerated individuals are inherently dangerous or untrustworthy. Instead, treat each person as an individual with their own unique experiences, strengths, and challenges. Similarly, avoid making assumptions about their educational level, job skills, or family support. Take the time to get to know them as individuals and to understand their specific needs and goals. By challenging your own biases and assumptions, you can create a more equitable and just environment that fosters trust and promotes successful re-entry.

Finally, building trust takes time, patience, and a genuine commitment to supporting individuals on their re-entry journey. There will be setbacks, challenges, and moments of frustration. It is important to remain steadfast in your commitment to building trust, even when faced with difficult situations. Remember that these individuals have often experienced trauma, abuse, and betrayal. It may take time for them to fully trust you and to believe that you are genuinely there to support them. Be patient, persistent, and empathetic. Celebrate their successes, acknowledge their struggles, and never give up on them. By consistently demonstrating your commitment to their well-being, you can build strong, trusting relationships that empower them to overcome the challenges of re-entry and to build a brighter future for themselves and their communities. Safety is equally crucial. By creating an environment that is physically and emotionally safe, you empower individuals to heal from past trauma, engage in the re-entry process, and build a foundation for a successful future.

3 Chapter 3: Education and Skill Development

Skill development and education represent a cornerstone of successful re-entry, providing a foundation upon which individuals can build stable and productive lives after incarceration. Assessing educational needs is paramount and requires a multifaceted approach. We can't assume that everyone has the same foundation, and we need to understand the individual's specific starting point. This can involve formal assessments like standardized tests to gauge reading, writing, and math skills. More importantly, informal conversations and interviews are invaluable. By listening to their stories, understanding their past educational experiences (both positive and negative), and identifying their goals, we can tailor educational plans that are both relevant and engaging. What are their aspirations? Do they dream of starting a business? Do they want to earn a specific certification? Aligning education with their aspirations dramatically increases motivation and persistence. Many individuals may have experienced disrupted schooling, learning disabilities, or a general disinterest in education during their earlier years. Therefore, a non-judgmental and supportive approach is crucial. We must create an environment where individuals feel comfortable admitting their knowledge gaps and confident in their ability to learn. This initial assessment is not simply about identifying deficits; it's about uncovering hidden strengths and identifying areas where they already possess knowledge or skills that can be built upon.

Vocational training offers a pathway to tangible skills and marketable credentials, and its impact should never be underestimated. The range of vocational training opportunities should be diverse and aligned with local labor market demands. This requires staying informed about the industries that are growing and the specific skills that employers are seeking. Options can include traditional trades such as carpentry, plumbing, and electrical work, which offer the possibility of self-employment or union membership. Emerging fields like renewable energy technology, computer programming, and healthcare support are also promising avenues. High-demand fields like truck driving or certified nursing assistant programs often provide faster entry into the workforce. The key is to offer training programs that are not only interesting but also lead to real job opportunities. Training programs should incorporate hands-on learning, simulations, and real-world projects to enhance skill development and ensure that individuals are prepared for the demands of the workplace. Mentorship opportunities with experienced professionals in the field can also be incredibly valuable, providing guidance, support, and networking connections. Crucially, vocational training should culminate in a recognized certification or credential that validates their skills and increases their marketability to employers. We must bridge the gap between the classroom and the workplace by fostering partnerships with local businesses. This can involve internships, apprenticeships, or even guaranteed job interviews upon successful completion of the training program. These partnerships benefit both the individuals seeking employment and the businesses in need of skilled workers, creating a mutually beneficial ecosystem.

Financial literacy is often overlooked but is essential for long-term stability. The ability to manage money effectively is a crucial life skill that empowers individuals to make informed financial decisions and avoid falling back into cycles of poverty or crime. Basic budgeting skills are vital. Many people lack a clear understanding of their income and expenses, leading to impulsive spending and debt accumulation. We need to teach them how to create a realistic budget, track their spending, and identify areas where they can save money. Understanding credit and debt management is equally important. Many individuals have damaged credit histories due to past financial mistakes. Educating them about how credit scores work, how to build or rebuild credit, and how to avoid predatory lending practices is essential. Learning about banking services is another crucial aspect of financial literacy. Many people lack access to or understanding of basic banking services such as checking accounts, savings accounts, and online banking. We need to help them open bank accounts, learn how to use them responsibly, and understand the fees and charges associated with these services. Planning for the future, even in small ways, is essential. Even if retirement seems distant, it's important to introduce the concept of saving for the future. This can involve opening a simple savings account or learning about basic investment options. We need to emphasize the importance of setting financial goals, such as saving for a down payment on a home, paying off debt, or starting a business. By empowering individuals with financial literacy skills, we equip them to take control of their finances, make informed decisions, and build a more secure future.

Effective job search strategies are paramount in a competitive market. Finding a job is not simply about submitting applications; it's about strategically marketing oneself to potential employers. The first step is to create a compelling resume and cover letter that highlights their skills, experience, and qualifications. Resume workshops can provide guidance on formatting, content, and tailoring resumes to specific job requirements. Mastering the art of interviewing is equally important. Mock interviews, where individuals can practice answering common interview questions and receive feedback on their performance, can be invaluable. They should be taught how to dress professionally, communicate effectively, and showcase their strengths and enthusiasm. Networking is also a crucial aspect of job searching. We need to help individuals build their professional networks by attending job fairs, connecting with people on LinkedIn, and reaching out to former colleagues or acquaintances. Even volunteering can be a great way to gain experience, build skills, and make connections. We should provide access to online job boards, career counseling services, and other resources that can assist them in their job search. Furthermore, we need to address potential barriers to employment, such as criminal records. Many employers are hesitant to hire individuals with criminal backgrounds, but there are resources and strategies available to help overcome this obstacle. This can involve expunging or sealing criminal records, obtaining certificates of rehabilitation, or disclosing their criminal history in a transparent and responsible manner.

Sustaining employment is the ultimate goal, so what can we do to make that happen? Landing a job is only the first step; retaining that job and building a successful career requires ongoing effort and commitment. Developing strong work habits is critical. This includes punctuality, attendance, reliability, and a positive attitude. We need to help individuals understand the importance of these qualities and how they contribute to their overall success. Effective communication and interpersonal skills are essential for building positive relationships with coworkers and supervisors. We can provide training in communication techniques, conflict resolution, and teamwork to enhance their ability to interact effectively in the workplace. Seeking mentorship and support is also important. Pairing individuals with experienced mentors who can provide guidance, support, and encouragement can significantly increase their chances of success. Access to ongoing counseling or support groups can also be beneficial, particularly for those who are struggling with personal challenges or adjusting to life outside of prison. Continued education and skill development are crucial for career advancement. We need to encourage individuals to pursue further education or training opportunities to enhance their skills and qualifications. This can involve taking online courses, attending workshops, or pursuing a degree or certification. We must emphasize the importance of setting career goals and developing a plan to achieve them. This can involve identifying their long-term aspirations, assessing their strengths and weaknesses, and creating a roadmap for career advancement. By providing ongoing support and resources, we can empower individuals to not only find jobs but also build fulfilling and sustainable careers.

3.1 Assessing Educational Needs

Understanding where an individual stands academically and professionally is the first, crucial step in crafting an effective re-entry plan. This process, assessment, goes beyond simply looking at diplomas or past job titles; it requires a deeper dive into their skills, knowledge gaps, and personal aspirations. A thorough assessment ensures that educational and vocational programs are tailored to meet their specific needs, maximizing their chances of success upon release.

Beginning with the fundamentals is vital. Many incarcerated individuals have had disrupted educational journeys or lacked access to quality education before incarceration. Standardized tests like the Test of Adult Basic Education (TABE) can provide a baseline understanding of their reading, math, and language skills. These assessments aren't about judging past failures but about pinpointing areas where foundational skills need strengthening. Perhaps an individual possesses practical skills but struggles with reading comprehension, hindering their ability to pass certification exams or understand complex work instructions. Addressing these fundamental gaps is paramount before moving on to more advanced training. I've seen individuals who were initially resistant to basic education thrive once they realized how these skills unlocked new opportunities.

Vocational aptitude is another critical area to explore. What are their innate talents and interests? What types of work do they find engaging and meaningful? Career aptitude tests, like the Strong Interest Inventory, can offer insights into potential career paths that align with their personalities and aptitudes. However, these tests are just a starting point. Practical assessments, such as hands-on workshops or shadowing experiences, can provide a more realistic understanding of whether a particular vocation is a good fit. It's essential to consider the job market in their intended location after release. Training in a high-demand field significantly increases their chances of finding employment. For instance, focusing on renewable energy jobs, healthcare support roles, or skilled trades (plumbing, electrical work) often provides a higher return on investment than training in fields with limited job opportunities. We want to provide skills that provide actual job placement!

Beyond formal education and vocational skills, assessing life skills is equally important. Many incarcerated individuals have limited experience managing finances, navigating bureaucratic systems, or resolving conflicts peacefully. A life skills assessment can identify areas where additional training is needed. This could include workshops on budgeting, credit repair, communication skills, and problem-solving. These skills are not just about finding a job; they're about building a stable and fulfilling life. Think about it, how can someone maintain employment if they can't manage their finances or resolve conflicts with coworkers?

Personal goals and aspirations must be considered within the whole of the assessment process. What do they hope to achieve upon release? What kind of life do they envision for themselves? Understanding their goals provides motivation and direction for their re-entry plan. Perhaps their dream is to start their own business, in this case, the focus should be on entrepreneurship training and access to resources for small business owners. Or maybe their priority is reconnecting with family, requiring them to provide family counseling and support services. Incorporating their aspirations into the re-entry plan increases their engagement and commitment to the process. I remember one individual who initially lacked motivation for vocational training until he realized it could help him provide a better life for his children.

Cultural and linguistic considerations cannot be overlooked. If an individual's primary language is not English, providing access to ESL classes and vocational training materials in their native language is crucial. Cultural sensitivity is also essential, as cultural background can influence communication styles, work ethic, and attitudes towards authority. Tailoring the assessment process and educational programs to be culturally relevant increases engagement and reduces barriers to learning.

The assessment process should be collaborative and empowering, not punitive or judgmental. It should involve open communication, active listening, and a genuine desire to understand the individual's needs and goals. Providing feedback in a constructive and supportive manner is essential. Let them know their strengths and areas for improvement, and work together to develop a plan that builds on their strengths and addresses their weaknesses. This collaborative approach fosters trust and encourages them to take ownership of their re-entry journey.

Regularly reviewing and updating the assessment is a key component, and this should be a continuous process, not a one-time event. As individuals progress through educational and vocational programs, their needs and goals may change. Regular assessments allow adjustments to be made to the re-entry plan, ensuring it remains relevant and effective. It also provides an opportunity to celebrate successes and address any challenges that may arise. This adaptability is crucial for maximizing their chances of a successful transition back into the community. This ensures that the support provided is always aligned with their current needs and aspirations, maximizing its effectiveness and promoting long-term success. Ultimately, it is not about simply providing education and training; it's about empowering them to become self-sufficient, responsible members of society.

3.2 Vocational Training Opportunities

The path to a fulfilling and productive life post-incarceration often hinges on acquiring marketable skills, and vocational training serves as a crucial bridge. It provides inmates with tangible skills, certifications, and experiences that can translate into employment opportunities upon release. This not only reduces recidivism but also empowers individuals to become self-sufficient and contributing members of society. Vocational training isn't just about learning a trade; it's about instilling a sense of purpose, boosting self-esteem,

and offering a legitimate pathway to economic independence. The landscape of available programs is surprisingly diverse, ranging from traditional trades like carpentry, plumbing, and electrical work to more modern fields like information technology, culinary arts, and healthcare support. The key is identifying programs that align with both individual aptitudes and the demands of the local job market.
Many correctional facilities offer in-house vocational training programs. These programs, tailored to the specific needs of the incarcerated population, provide a structured learning environment and hands-on experience. For example, a prison might offer a certified welding program, a culinary arts course leading to a food handler's certification, or a construction trades program that builds prefabricated homes. The advantage of these in-house programs is their accessibility and affordability; inmates typically don't have to pay tuition, and the programs are designed to fit within the constraints of the prison environment. Moreover, they often incorporate life skills training, such as resume writing, interview skills, and financial literacy, which are essential for successful re-entry. It's crucial to research the accreditation and reputation of these programs, ensuring that the skills learned are recognized and valued by potential employers. A well-regarded in-house program can provide a solid foundation for future employment.

Beyond the walls of correctional facilities, community colleges and technical schools often partner with prisons to offer vocational training courses. These partnerships provide inmates with access to a broader range of programs and instructors with specialized expertise. For instance, a community college might offer a computer programming course, a healthcare assistant certification program, or an automotive repair course within the prison. These programs often lead to industry-recognized certifications or associate degrees, significantly enhancing employment prospects. The challenge, however, lies in bridging the gap between completing the program while incarcerated and finding employment upon release. It's essential to establish connections with potential employers and support organizations before release to ensure a smooth transition. Community college partnerships can be a game-changer, providing access to high-quality education and valuable credentials.

Apprenticeship programs represent a unique opportunity to "earn while you learn." These programs combine on-the-job training with classroom instruction, allowing inmates to develop skills under the guidance of experienced professionals. For example, an inmate might participate in an apprenticeship program in carpentry, electrical work, or plumbing, working alongside skilled tradespeople and earning a wage while learning the trade. These programs typically last for several years and culminate in a nationally recognized certification. While access to apprenticeship programs within correctional facilities can be limited, there are organizations that work to connect formerly incarcerated individuals with apprenticeship opportunities upon release. The benefits of apprenticeship programs are numerous: they provide hands-on experience, a steady income, and a clear pathway to a skilled trade. Furthermore, they often lead to long-term employment with a reputable company.

Securing funding for vocational training can be a significant hurdle for inmates. Many are indigent and lack the resources to pay for tuition, books, and other expenses. Fortunately, there are several funding sources available. Government grants, such as Pell Grants and Workforce Innovation and Opportunity Act (WIOA) funds, can be used to cover the costs of vocational training programs. Additionally, many non-profit organizations offer scholarships and financial assistance to formerly incarcerated individuals seeking to improve their skills and find employment. It's essential to research and apply for these funding opportunities well in advance of release. Furthermore, some employers offer tuition reimbursement programs for employees who pursue further education or training. Connecting with potential employers before release can open doors to these opportunities. Don't overlook the power of crowdfunding and online fundraising platforms to solicit support from friends, family, and community members.

The most effective vocational training programs are those that are tailored to the individual's needs and interests. It's essential to conduct a thorough assessment of each inmate's skills, aptitudes, and career goals. This assessment should consider factors such as prior work experience, educational background, and personal interests. Based on this assessment, a customized training plan can be developed that aligns with the individual's strengths and the demands of the local job market. This might involve enrolling in a specific vocational training program, participating in an apprenticeship, or pursuing a college degree. The key is to create a plan that is both realistic and ambitious, providing a clear pathway to a fulfilling and productive career.

Ultimately, the success of vocational training depends on providing comprehensive support services to inmates both during and after incarceration. This includes access to career counseling, job placement assistance, and mentoring programs. Career counselors can help inmates identify suitable training programs, develop job search strategies, and prepare for interviews. Job placement assistance can connect inmates with potential employers and provide support in securing employment. Mentoring programs can provide ongoing support and guidance, helping formerly incarcerated individuals navigate the challenges of re-entry and build successful careers. A strong support network is essential for overcoming the barriers to employment and achieving long-term success.

The skills acquired through vocational training are more than just tools for a job; they are instruments of transformation, enabling individuals to reshape their lives and contribute positively to their communities. It's an investment not only in the individual but also in a safer and more prosperous society for everyone.

3.3 Financial Literacy Essentials

Financial stability is the bedrock of successful re-entry; without it, the challenges multiply exponentially, increasing the risk of recidivism. Therefore, grasping the essentials of financial literacy isn't just about managing money; it's about building a future, a future where self-sufficiency and responsible decision-making replace the despair and instability that often lead to incarceration. Let's begin.

Understanding your current financial standing is the crucial first step. This means creating a detailed picture of your income, expenses, assets, and debts. It's not always easy to face the reality of your finances, especially after a period of incarceration, but transparency is key. Start by listing all sources of income, whether it's from employment, assistance programs, or any other means. Then, meticulously track your expenses, categorizing them into necessities like housing, food, transportation, and healthcare, and discretionary items. Consider using budgeting apps, spreadsheets, or even a simple notebook to monitor your spending habits. Once you have a clear overview of your financial situation, you can begin to identify areas where you can cut back on expenses and allocate resources more effectively. This foundation of self-awareness is paramount for setting realistic financial goals and achieving long-term stability.

Budgeting is the cornerstone of financial management, providing a roadmap for allocating your resources and achieving your financial goals. A budget isn't about restriction; it's about empowerment, allowing you to make informed choices about where your money goes. Start by allocating funds to essential needs such as housing, food, and transportation. Be realistic about these expenses; underestimate them and your budget will quickly fall apart. Next, allocate funds to debt repayment. This is often a significant challenge for individuals re-entering society, but prioritizing debt repayment is essential for improving your credit score and reducing financial stress. Finally, allocate funds for savings and discretionary spending. Even small amounts saved consistently can make a big difference over time. Be sure to review your budget regularly and make adjustments as needed. As your income changes or your financial goals evolve, your budget should adapt accordingly.

Credit scores are often perceived as mysterious numbers, but they play a crucial role in accessing financial products and services, from loans and credit cards to housing and employment. Understanding how credit scores work is essential for building or rebuilding your credit history. Your credit score is primarily based on your payment history, credit utilization, length of credit history, types of credit used, and new credit inquiries. Late payments can have a significant negative impact on your credit score, so it's crucial to pay your bills on time, every time. Credit utilization refers to the amount of credit you're using compared to your total credit limit. Aim to keep your credit utilization below 30% to avoid negatively impacting your credit score. If you have a limited credit history, consider opening a secured credit card or becoming an authorized user on someone else's credit card to begin building your credit. Be patient and persistent; it takes time to build a positive credit history, but the rewards are well worth the effort.

Debt management is a critical aspect of financial literacy, particularly for individuals re-entering society who may face pre-existing debts or encounter new financial challenges. High-interest debt, such as credit card debt or payday loans, can quickly spiral out of control if not managed effectively. Start by prioritizing your debts, focusing on paying off those with the highest interest rates first. Consider consolidating your debts into a single loan with a lower interest rate, or exploring options for debt forgiveness or debt management plans. Avoid taking on new debt unless absolutely necessary, and be wary of predatory lenders who may try to take advantage of your situation. Seek advice from a reputable financial counselor or credit counseling agency to develop a personalized debt management plan that meets your specific needs and circumstances. Remember, it's a marathon, not a sprint.

Savings are the cornerstone of financial security, providing a buffer against unexpected expenses and enabling you to achieve your long-term financial goals. Start by setting realistic savings goals, whether it's saving for a down payment on a home, building an emergency fund, or investing for retirement. Aim to save a small percentage of your income each month, even if it's just a few dollars. Consider automating your savings by setting up automatic transfers from your checking account to your savings account. Explore different savings options, such as high-yield savings accounts, certificates of deposit (CDs), or money market accounts, to maximize your returns. Be disciplined and consistent with your savings efforts, and resist the temptation to dip into your savings for non-essential expenses.

Investing can seem daunting, but it's a powerful tool for building wealth over time. Start by educating yourself about the different types of investments, such as stocks, bonds, mutual funds, and real estate. Consider your risk tolerance, investment goals, and time horizon when choosing investments. Diversify your portfolio to reduce risk by investing in a variety of asset classes and sectors. If you're new to investing, consider starting with low-cost index funds or exchange-traded funds (ETFs), which provide broad market exposure at a low cost. Consult with a qualified financial advisor to develop an investment strategy that aligns with your financial goals and risk tolerance.

Protecting yourself from financial scams and fraud is essential for maintaining financial security. Be wary of unsolicited offers or opportunities that seem too good to be true. Never give out personal or financial information over the phone or online unless you're certain you're dealing with a reputable company or organization. Monitor your credit report regularly for signs of identity theft or fraudulent activity. Be cautious of phishing scams, which are designed to trick you into revealing your personal information. Report any suspected scams or fraud to the appropriate authorities, such as the Federal Trade Commission (FTC) or your local law enforcement agency.

Financial literacy is a lifelong journey, not a destination. As your financial situation evolves and your goals change, it's essential to continue learning and growing your financial knowledge. Take advantage of free resources, such as online courses, workshops, and seminars, to expand your understanding of personal finance topics. Read books, articles, and blogs about personal finance to stay informed about current trends and best practices. Seek advice from qualified financial professionals, such as financial advisors, accountants, and attorneys, to get personalized guidance tailored to your specific needs and circumstances. By committing to lifelong learning, you can empower yourself to make informed financial decisions and achieve your financial goals.

3.4 Job Search Strategies

Landing a job after incarceration presents unique hurdles, but with a strategic approach, these challenges can be overcome. It is a critical component of successful re-entry, fostering financial independence, self-esteem, and a sense of purpose. Let's delve into practical strategies to navigate the job market effectively.

First, recognize your marketable skills. Don't underestimate the skills you've acquired during your time in custody. Many tasks within correctional facilities require discipline, teamwork, problem-solving, and attention to detail. Did you work in the kitchen? That's experience in food preparation and hygiene. Were you involved in facility maintenance? You've gained skills in basic repairs and upkeep. Actively identify these skills and think about how they translate to civilian jobs. For example, organizational skills honed in managing your daily schedule can be framed as time management expertise. Similarly, conflict resolution skills developed in a challenging environment are highly valued in many workplaces. I know that often, people don't see the transferable value right away, but trust me, it's there. It's also crucial to be honest with yourself about skill gaps. Identify areas where you need additional training or certification and start exploring options for addressing them.

Crafting a compelling resume is non-negotiable. Honesty is crucial, but the way you present your history matters. You are not necessarily required to disclose your entire criminal record upfront unless specifically asked on the application. However, if you choose to disclose, or if a background check will reveal it, be prepared to address it proactively and positively. Frame your experience in a way that highlights your rehabilitation and commitment to a productive future. Focus on the skills you've gained, the programs you've completed, and any positive changes you've made. A skills-based resume is often a good option, allowing you to emphasize your abilities rather than focusing on chronological work history. Include any educational achievements, certifications, or vocational training. Use action verbs to describe your responsibilities and accomplishments, and quantify your achievements whenever possible. Proofread meticulously for errors in grammar and spelling; even minor mistakes can create a negative impression. If you are unsure about how to present yourself, seek assistance from a re-entry organization or career counselor specializing in working with formerly incarcerated individuals.

Networking is your secret weapon. Don't underestimate the power of personal connections. Reach out to family, friends, and community organizations. Inform them of your job search and the types of opportunities you are seeking. Attend job fairs, community events, and workshops, even if they seem intimidating. Prepare a brief "elevator pitch" summarizing your skills and experience. Practice introducing yourself and making a positive impression. Network with people who work in fields you're interested in, even if they don't have immediate job openings. Ask for informational interviews to learn more about their careers and get advice on breaking into the industry. Many employers are willing to give someone a chance if they demonstrate genuine enthusiasm and a strong work ethic. Remember, it's often about who you know, not just what you know.

Master the art of interviewing. This is your chance to shine and demonstrate your potential. Prepare for common interview questions, including those about your past. Be honest and concise in your responses, and focus on what you've learned from your experiences. Practice answering difficult questions with a calm and confident demeanor. Research the company and the position you're applying for. Show that you understand their mission and values, and explain how your skills and experience align with their needs. Dress professionally, arrive on time, and maintain eye contact. Send a thank-you note after the interview to reiterate your interest and express your appreciation for their time. Remember that your interview starts from the moment you walk in the door.

Don't give up. Job searching can be discouraging, especially with a criminal record. You will likely face rejection. Don't let it deter you. Stay persistent, continue to refine your resume and interviewing skills, and broaden your network. Seek out support from re-entry organizations, mentors, and counselors. Celebrate small victories along the way, and remember that every setback is a learning opportunity. There are resources available to help you succeed. Take advantage of them. Many organizations specialize in providing job training, placement assistance, and legal support to formerly incarcerated individuals. These programs can offer valuable skills development, job leads, and guidance through the complexities of the re-entry process. Explore government initiatives, such as the Work Opportunity Tax Credit (WOTC), which incentivizes employers to hire individuals with criminal records.

3.5 Sustaining Employment

Landing a job is one thing; keeping it is another. Many individuals returning from incarceration face unique hurdles in sustaining employment, often stemming from a combination of personal challenges, systemic biases, and the sheer pressure of reintegration. Therefore, it's critical to equip them with the right tools and strategies, extending beyond initial job placement to foster long-term success.

One of the most significant obstacles is simply the stigma associated with a criminal record. Many employers, even those willing to give someone a second chance, harbor reservations about reliability, trustworthiness, and potential workplace disruptions. It's also sometimes seen as a danger to their reputation. Overcoming this requires proactive transparency and demonstrating a commitment to personal growth. I advise individuals to be prepared to address their past directly, honestly, and without making excuses. Frame the experience as a turning point, highlighting the lessons learned, the skills gained (even within the correctional setting), and the proactive steps taken to rehabilitate and become a productive member of society. Honesty can actually build trust, but it must be accompanied by clear evidence of positive change and a genuine desire to contribute. This conversation is never easy, and that's precisely why practicing this explanation beforehand – perhaps with a mentor or counselor – is so essential.

Beyond stigma, practical challenges often derail early employment opportunities. Lack of reliable transportation is a huge issue for many, especially in areas with limited public transportation. I have seen this problem cause tardiness, absenteeism, and eventual job loss. Similarly, unstable housing creates constant stress and uncertainty, making it difficult to focus on work. Childcare responsibilities, especially for single parents, present another significant hurdle. Without dependable childcare, maintaining a consistent work schedule becomes nearly impossible. Addressing these basic needs is often a prerequisite for sustainable employment. Connecting individuals with resources like transportation assistance programs, affordable housing initiatives, and childcare subsidies can make a tangible difference in their ability to retain their jobs. I often suggest exploring carpooling options with coworkers or seeking assistance from local charities. The goal is to proactively mitigate these potential disruptions before they jeopardize employment.

Developing strong workplace skills is also paramount. Many individuals entering or re-entering the workforce lack essential soft skills like communication, teamwork, problem-solving, and conflict resolution. These skills are just as important as technical abilities, if not more so, for long-term job success. Employers consistently report that deficiencies in these areas are a primary reason for employee termination. Providing targeted training in these areas is crucial. Role-playing scenarios, group projects, and mentorship programs can help individuals develop and refine these skills in a supportive environment. Equally important is teaching effective communication strategies for addressing workplace conflicts constructively and professionally. Learning to give and receive feedback, navigate disagreements, and resolve issues collaboratively can significantly improve workplace relationships and job stability.

Moreover, financial literacy is fundamental. Managing finances effectively is critical for stability and reducing stress, which in turn positively impacts job performance. Many individuals lack the basic skills to budget, save, manage debt, and make sound financial decisions. Providing financial literacy workshops can equip them with the tools to control their finances, avoid debt traps, and build a secure financial future. I recommend emphasizing practical skills such as creating a budget, tracking expenses, and setting financial goals. Additionally, providing information on accessing affordable banking services, understanding credit scores, and avoiding predatory lending practices can empower individuals to make informed financial choices. This will reduce stress, and increase focus at work, greatly increasing the chances of keeping a job.

Furthermore, building a strong support network is indispensable. The transition back into society can be isolating and overwhelming. Having a support system of family, friends, mentors, and community organizations can provide emotional support, practical assistance, and encouragement. Mentorship programs, in particular, can be invaluable in providing guidance, accountability, and a positive role model. I've found that connecting individuals with mentors who have successfully navigated similar challenges can be incredibly motivating and inspiring. Support groups, both within and outside the workplace, can also provide a sense of community and shared experience, reducing feelings of isolation and promoting resilience. These networks must understand the reality of re-entry, and be prepared to provide concrete, specific help.

Self-care strategies also play a vital role. The stress of re-entry, coupled with the demands of a new job, can take a toll on mental and physical health. Teaching healthy coping mechanisms for managing stress, anxiety, and triggers is essential. Mindfulness exercises, relaxation techniques, and regular physical activity can help individuals maintain emotional balance and prevent burnout. Encouraging them to prioritize self-care, even in small ways, can significantly improve their overall well-being and job performance. It's about helping them create a sustainable lifestyle, not just landing a job. Remember, sustainable employment is not just about finding a job, it's about equipping individuals with the skills, resources, and support they need to thrive in the workplace and beyond. By addressing the multifaceted challenges they face, we can empower them to break the cycle of recidivism and build successful, fulfilling lives.

Finally, remember the importance of ongoing support. Re-entry is not a one-time event; it's an ongoing process. Providing continued support and resources, even after initial job placement, is essential for long-term success. This can include regular check-ins with mentors, access to ongoing training and development opportunities, and assistance with navigating workplace challenges. By providing sustained support, we can demonstrate a commitment to their success and help them overcome the inevitable hurdles that arise along the way.

4 Chapter 4: Mental Health and Well-being

Mental health significantly impacts successful re-entry. It's a cornerstone of stability, influencing everything from employment to relationships. Many individuals leaving incarceration have pre-existing mental health conditions, often exacerbated by the prison experience itself. It's vital to understand this and address it proactively.

Accessing mental health services can be a significant hurdle. Within correctional facilities, resources are often limited, and the quality of care can vary greatly. It is important to advocate for comprehensive mental health screenings and treatment options during incarceration, not just as release approaches. This might involve individual therapy, group counseling, medication management, or a combination of these approaches. Connecting inmates with these services before their release is key. Prepare them for the transition to community-based care by identifying potential providers, assisting with insurance applications (if applicable), and scheduling initial appointments. Create a "warm handoff" – a direct connection between the inmate and a community-based provider – can significantly improve the likelihood of continued treatment. Furthermore, educate inmates about their rights regarding mental health care and how to navigate the system upon release. This includes understanding insurance options, accessing local mental health agencies, and knowing their rights regarding confidentiality and treatment.

Managing stress and anxiety is crucial for individuals transitioning back into society. The re-entry process is inherently stressful, involving numerous challenges such as finding housing, securing employment, and rebuilding relationships. Without effective coping mechanisms, stress and anxiety can lead to relapse, substance abuse, and re-incarceration. Practical strategies can be taught, such as mindfulness techniques. Mindfulness involves focusing on the present moment without judgment, which can help reduce racing thoughts and promote relaxation. Simple exercises like deep breathing, meditation, and body scan meditations can be easily learned and practiced. Another essential tool is cognitive restructuring. This involves identifying and challenging negative thought patterns that contribute to stress and anxiety. Individuals can learn to reframe their thoughts in a more positive and realistic way, reducing their emotional distress. Lifestyle changes also play a vital role. Regular exercise, a balanced diet, and sufficient sleep can significantly improve mood and reduce stress levels. Encourage inmates to develop healthy habits during incarceration and to continue them upon release. It's important also to educate on the importance of self-care. Self-care involves engaging in activities that promote well-being, such as spending time in nature, pursuing hobbies, or connecting with loved ones.

Building resilience is the cornerstone of long-term success. Resilience is the ability to bounce back from adversity, adapt to challenges, and maintain a positive outlook despite difficulties. It is not an innate trait but rather a skill that can be developed over time. To foster resilience, it's necessary to focus on building strong social support networks. Isolation can exacerbate mental health challenges, making it crucial for individuals to connect with others who can provide emotional support, practical assistance, and a sense of belonging. These networks can include family members, friends, mentors, support groups, and faith-based communities. Also, promoting a sense of purpose and meaning in life is vital. Having a clear sense of purpose can provide motivation, direction, and a sense of hope, even in the face of adversity. This might involve setting goals, pursuing passions, engaging in volunteer work, or finding a career that aligns with their values. Furthermore, teaching problem-solving skills is key. Resilience involves the ability to effectively cope with challenges and find solutions to problems. Individuals can learn to break down complex problems into smaller, manageable steps, identify potential resources, and develop action plans. Celebrating small victories and focusing on personal strengths is also necessary. It's important to acknowledge and celebrate progress, no matter how small. Focusing on personal strengths and past successes can boost confidence and remind individuals of their capabilities.

In conclusion, supporting the mental health and well-being of individuals re-entering society is paramount. It requires a multi-faceted approach that includes access to quality mental health services, strategies for managing stress and anxiety, and interventions to build resilience. By prioritizing mental health, we can significantly improve the chances of successful re-entry and reduce recidivism, leading to safer and healthier communities. Remember that consistent encouragement and a supportive environment are crucial throughout this process.

4.1 Accessing Mental Health Services

Navigating the mental healthcare system can feel like traversing a labyrinth, particularly for individuals re-entering society after incarceration. The system is often complex, fragmented, and challenging to access, presenting numerous hurdles that can significantly impact successful reintegration. Understanding these challenges and knowing how to navigate the system is paramount for ensuring that returning citizens receive the support they need to thrive.

One of the first major hurdles is simply knowing where to start. Many individuals leaving incarceration are unaware of the mental health resources available to them in the community. This lack of awareness is often compounded by limited access to information while incarcerated and a general distrust of the healthcare system, especially within marginalized communities. To address this, proactive measures are necessary. Correctional facilities should provide comprehensive pre-release planning that includes detailed information on local mental health providers, community mental health centers, and support groups. This information should be provided in multiple formats, including written materials, videos, and one-on-one counseling sessions, ensuring accessibility for individuals with varying literacy levels. Furthermore, establishing partnerships between correctional facilities and community-based organizations can facilitate a seamless transition by connecting individuals with services before their release. These organizations can provide ongoing support, advocacy, and navigation assistance, helping individuals overcome barriers to accessing care.

The financial burden of mental healthcare is another significant barrier. Many individuals leaving incarceration lack the resources to afford therapy, medication, or other necessary services. Even with insurance, co-pays and deductibles can be prohibitive. Fortunately, several options can help mitigate these financial challenges. Medicaid is a government-funded healthcare program that provides coverage to low-income individuals and families. Applying for Medicaid upon

release is crucial, as it can significantly reduce the cost of mental healthcare. Additionally, many community mental health centers offer services on a sliding fee scale, meaning that the cost of care is adjusted based on an individual's income. These centers often provide a range of services, including therapy, medication management, and case management, making them a valuable resource for those with limited financial means. Another avenue to explore is pharmaceutical assistance programs offered by drug manufacturers. These programs provide free or discounted medications to individuals who meet certain income requirements. Navigating these programs can be complex, but case managers and social workers can provide assistance in completing applications and gathering necessary documentation.
Even when individuals are aware of available resources and can afford them, bureaucratic hurdles can further complicate access to care. Lengthy waitlists, complicated application processes, and strict eligibility requirements can discourage individuals from seeking help. Addressing these challenges requires systemic changes. Mental health providers should streamline their intake processes, making it easier for individuals to access care. This may involve simplifying paperwork, offering online registration options, and providing flexible appointment scheduling. Furthermore, advocating for policies that expand access to mental healthcare is essential. This includes increasing funding for community mental health centers, reducing administrative burdens, and expanding Medicaid eligibility. Building relationships with local policymakers and advocating for legislative changes can help create a more accessible and equitable mental healthcare system.

The stigma associated with mental illness is a pervasive barrier that prevents many individuals from seeking help. This stigma is often amplified for individuals with a history of incarceration, who may fear judgment and discrimination from healthcare providers, employers, and their communities. Overcoming this stigma requires a multifaceted approach. Public awareness campaigns can help educate the public about mental illness and promote understanding and acceptance. These campaigns can feature stories from individuals who have successfully managed their mental health, demonstrating that recovery is possible. Additionally, creating safe and supportive spaces where individuals can share their experiences without fear of judgment is crucial. Support groups and peer-led programs can provide a sense of community and belonging, helping individuals feel less alone in their struggles. Furthermore, mental health providers should be trained to provide culturally competent care, recognizing the unique challenges and experiences of individuals from diverse backgrounds. The importance of culturally competent care cannot be overstated. Individuals from marginalized communities often face unique challenges in accessing mental healthcare, including language barriers, cultural differences, and a lack of trust in the healthcare system. Culturally competent providers are aware of these challenges and tailor their services to meet the specific needs of their clients. This may involve providing services in multiple languages, incorporating cultural values and beliefs into treatment plans, and building trust by demonstrating empathy and respect. Furthermore, engaging community leaders and organizations can help bridge the gap between mental health providers and the communities they serve. These leaders can act as trusted messengers, promoting mental health awareness and encouraging individuals to seek help.

Finally, remember that seeking mental health support is a sign of strength, not weakness. Re-entry can be an incredibly challenging process, and it is normal to experience stress, anxiety, and other mental health concerns. Don't hesitate to reach out for help when you need it. There are people who care about you and want to support you on your journey. Building a strong support network, practicing self-care, and seeking professional help when needed are all essential components of a successful and fulfilling life.

4.2 Managing Stress and Anxiety

Stress and anxiety. These are constant companions for many individuals re-entering society after incarceration. The weight of the past, the uncertainty of the future, and the daily struggles of navigating a changed world can feel overwhelming. Learning to manage these powerful emotions is not a luxury; it's an essential survival skill that can pave the way for successful reintegration. Consider stress as the body's natural reaction to demands or threats, and anxiety as a persistent feeling of worry or unease. For those transitioning out of prison, these feelings are often amplified due to the multitude of challenges they face.

The first step towards managing stress and anxiety is recognizing the triggers. What situations, thoughts, or interactions consistently lead to feelings of unease or overwhelm? For some, it might be the prospect of job interviews, triggering fears of rejection and inadequacy. For others, it could be interactions with law enforcement, stirring up past trauma and feelings of powerlessness. Identifying these specific triggers is crucial because it allows you to develop targeted coping strategies. This involves introspection, perhaps journaling to document your feelings and the events surrounding them. A therapist or counselor can provide guidance in uncovering deeper patterns and understanding the root causes of your stress and anxiety. Don't underestimate the power of self-awareness; it's the foundation upon which effective management strategies are built.

Once you know your triggers, you can start to implement proactive strategies. One highly effective technique is mindfulness. This isn't about emptying your mind entirely, but rather about paying attention to the present moment without judgment. This can involve focusing on your breath, noticing the sensations in your body, or simply observing your thoughts as they pass by. Start with short mindfulness exercises, even just five minutes a day. You can find guided meditations online or through apps. The goal is to cultivate a sense of calm and centeredness, allowing you to respond to stressful situations with greater clarity and control. Think of it as building a mental muscle that gets stronger with practice. Consistent mindfulness helps create space between your thoughts and your reactions, preventing impulsive behavior driven by anxiety.

Beyond mindfulness, prioritize physical well-being. Exercise is a powerful stress reliever. Physical activity releases endorphins, which have mood-boosting effects. It doesn't have to be anything strenuous; a brisk walk, a bike ride, or even dancing to your favorite music can make a difference. Equally important is getting enough sleep. Sleep deprivation can exacerbate anxiety and make it harder to cope with stress. Aim for at least seven to eight hours of quality sleep each night. Establish a regular sleep schedule, create a relaxing bedtime routine, and avoid caffeine and alcohol before bed. Nutrition also plays a vital role. A balanced diet provides the nutrients your body needs to function optimally, including regulating mood and energy levels. Limit processed foods, sugary drinks, and excessive caffeine, as these can contribute to anxiety and mood swings. Instead, focus on whole foods like fruits, vegetables, lean proteins, and whole grains. Nourishing your body is an act of self-care that can significantly impact your mental well-being.

Building a strong support system is another crucial component of managing stress and anxiety. Isolation can worsen these feelings, while having trusted individuals to confide in can provide invaluable emotional support. This could include family members, friends, mentors, or support groups specifically designed for individuals re-entering society. Sharing your experiences with others who understand what you're going through can reduce feelings of shame and isolation. Support groups also offer a safe space to learn coping strategies from others and gain a sense of community. If you don't have a natural support network, actively seek one out. Look for community organizations, faith-based groups, or online forums where you can connect with others who share similar experiences. Remember, you don't have to go through this alone.

Furthermore, developing effective problem-solving skills can help reduce anxiety by addressing the underlying causes of stress. Break down overwhelming problems into smaller, more manageable steps. Identify the resources available to you and seek assistance when needed. Don't be afraid to ask for help from social workers, counselors, or community organizations. Learning to advocate for yourself and navigate complex systems is a valuable skill that can empower you to overcome challenges and reduce feelings of powerlessness. Sometimes, anxiety stems from feeling like you're not in control of your life. By taking proactive steps to address your problems, you regain a sense of agency and reduce the feeling of being overwhelmed.

Finally, consider seeking professional help if your stress and anxiety are significantly impacting your daily life. A therapist or counselor can provide evidence-based therapies like cognitive behavioral therapy (CBT) or dialectical behavior therapy (DBT), which can help you identify and change negative thought patterns and develop coping skills. Medication may also be an option for some individuals, but it should be discussed with a qualified healthcare professional.

There is no shame in seeking help. It's a sign of strength, not weakness, to recognize when you need support. Mental health is just as important as physical health, and seeking professional help is a sign of self-care and a commitment to your well-being. Remember that managing stress and anxiety is an ongoing process, not a one-time fix. There will be good days and bad days. Be patient with yourself, celebrate small victories, and don't give up on your journey towards a more peaceful and fulfilling life. Re-entry is a marathon, not a sprint.

4.3 Building Resilience

Resilience is not simply bouncing back; it's about adapting and growing stronger in the face of adversity. For individuals re-entering society after incarceration, the road ahead is often fraught with challenges – unemployment, social stigma, strained family relationships, and the ever-present risk of relapse. Cultivating resilience becomes a vital skill, a shield against the storms that threaten to derail their progress. It is a muscle that needs consistent exercise and targeted training.

Building resilience isn't a one-size-fits-all process. It requires a personalized approach that considers individual strengths, experiences, and support systems. We need to move away from the notion of resilience as an innate trait and view it as a collection of skills and habits that can be developed and strengthened over time. This begins with self-awareness. Encourage individuals to identify their personal strengths – what are they good at? What have they overcome in the past? Recognizing these strengths can provide a foundation of self-belief upon which to build further resilience. Furthermore, understanding their vulnerabilities – what triggers stress or anxiety? What are their weaknesses? – allows them to develop coping mechanisms and strategies to mitigate potential setbacks. Journaling, mindfulness exercises, and discussions with trusted counselors or mentors can all contribute to this process of self-discovery.

Creating a supportive network is also paramount. Isolation is a major risk factor for recidivism and can significantly hinder the development of resilience. Connecting with family members (where appropriate and safe), building relationships with prosocial peers, and engaging with community support groups can provide a sense of belonging and shared experience. These networks offer a safe space to share challenges, receive encouragement, and access practical support. The emphasis here should be on quality over quantity. A few strong, supportive relationships are far more beneficial than a large network of superficial acquaintances. Moreover, consider the role of mentors. Pairing individuals with positive role models who have overcome similar challenges can provide invaluable guidance and inspiration. Mentors can offer practical advice, share their own experiences of navigating the re-entry process, and provide ongoing support and accountability.

Effective coping mechanisms are essential for navigating the inevitable stressors of re-entry. These mechanisms can range from practical problem-solving strategies to emotional regulation techniques. Teach individuals to break down large, overwhelming problems into smaller, more manageable steps. Encourage them to focus on what they can control and to let go of what they cannot. Mindfulness practices, such as meditation and deep breathing exercises, can help individuals to manage stress and anxiety in the moment. Regular physical activity, a healthy diet, and sufficient sleep are also crucial for maintaining mental and emotional well-being. Crucially, equip individuals with relapse prevention strategies. This involves identifying triggers – people, places, or situations that increase the risk of returning to harmful behaviors – and developing plans to avoid or manage those triggers. It also means recognizing the early warning signs of relapse and having a clear plan of action to seek help when needed. Relapse is not a failure; it's a setback. Help individuals to view it as an opportunity to learn and grow, and to reaffirm their commitment to a positive future.

Goal setting is another key component of building resilience. Having clear, achievable goals provides a sense of purpose and direction, and helps individuals to stay focused on their long-term objectives. Encourage individuals to set both short-term and long-term goals in various areas of their lives – employment, education, family, health, and personal growth. Make sure that these goals are SMART: Specific, Measurable, Achievable, Relevant, and Time-bound. Celebrate small victories along the way. Acknowledging progress, no matter how small, can boost morale and reinforce positive behaviors. This could involve anything from completing a job application to attending a support group meeting to staying sober for a week.

Challenging negative thinking patterns is crucial. Many individuals re-entering society struggle with self-doubt, feelings of hopelessness, and negative beliefs about their ability to succeed. Cognitive restructuring techniques, such as identifying and challenging negative thoughts, can help individuals to develop a more positive and realistic outlook. Encourage them to focus on their strengths, accomplishments, and potential for growth. Help them to reframe setbacks as learning opportunities rather than as evidence of failure. Promote self-compassion. Many individuals are harder on themselves than they are on others. Encourage them to treat themselves with the same kindness and understanding that they would offer to a friend facing similar challenges. This involves acknowledging their pain, recognizing their common humanity, and offering themselves words of encouragement and support.

Finally, foster a sense of purpose and meaning. Connecting with something larger than oneself can provide a powerful source of resilience. This could involve volunteering in the community, pursuing a creative passion, engaging in spiritual practices, or advocating for a cause they believe in. Encourage individuals to explore their values and to identify activities that align with those values. Help them to find ways to contribute to their communities and to make a positive difference in the lives of others. This sense of purpose can provide a sense of hope and motivation, even in the face of adversity. Resilience isn't about avoiding hardship; it's about developing the inner strength and resources to navigate it successfully. It is a lifelong journey, not a destination. As individuals continue to face challenges and setbacks, they will continue to learn and grow, and their resilience will become even stronger.

5 Chapter 5: Family and Social Connections

Re-entering society after incarceration is rarely a solitary journey; it is intricately woven with the threads of family and social connections. These relationships, whether strained or supportive, profoundly influence an individual's ability to reintegrate successfully. My experience working with returning citizens has consistently highlighted the pivotal role of these connections, serving as either a bedrock of support or a source of significant stress and potential relapse. The aim is to foster healthy, positive relationships that contribute to a stable and fulfilling life.

Rebuilding family relationships is often the most challenging aspect of re-entry. Years of separation, broken trust, and shifting family dynamics can create deep rifts. Initial interactions may be fraught with anxiety, resentment, or unrealistic expectations. The incarcerated individual may feel like an outsider, struggling to find their place within the family structure. Family members, in turn, may harbor anger, fear, or uncertainty about the returning individual's ability to adapt and contribute positively. Open and honest communication is crucial, but it must be approached with patience and empathy. Facilitating family therapy or mediation can provide a structured environment to address underlying issues, establish clear boundaries, and foster understanding. It is equally vital to manage expectations realistically. Rebuilding trust takes time, and setbacks are inevitable. Acknowledge the pain and hurt caused by past actions, but focus on building a foundation for a healthier future. Forgiveness, both offered and received, is a powerful tool for healing, but it must be genuine and not used as a means to avoid accountability.

The definition of 'family' may need to be broadened. For some, biological family relationships are irreparably damaged or simply nonexistent. In these cases, creating a "chosen family" of supportive friends, mentors, or community members can be just as valuable. These individuals can provide the emotional support, practical assistance, and sense of belonging that are essential for successful reentry. Encouraging involvement in community groups, religious organizations, or recreational activities can facilitate the development of these connections. Mentorship programs, pairing returning citizens with positive role models, can offer guidance, encouragement, and a sense of accountability.

Developing healthy romantic relationships requires careful consideration. Individuals who have been incarcerated may have limited experience with healthy relationship dynamics, and may struggle with intimacy, communication, and conflict resolution. It is essential to address any underlying issues related to domestic violence, substance abuse, or unhealthy relationship patterns before entering into a new romantic relationship. Focusing on self-improvement, building self-esteem, and developing healthy coping mechanisms are crucial steps. Furthermore, it's important to be transparent with potential partners about one's past, while also emphasizing a commitment to change and a desire for a healthy, respectful relationship. Pre-marital counseling or relationship skills workshops can provide valuable tools and guidance.

Navigating social stigma is an ever-present challenge for returning citizens. The label of "ex-offender" can create barriers to employment, housing, and social acceptance. Societal prejudice can lead to feelings of isolation, shame, and despair. While it is impossible to completely eliminate social stigma, there are strategies for mitigating its impact. One approach is to focus on building a strong support network of individuals who are accepting and non-judgmental. Connecting with other returning citizens can provide a sense of camaraderie and shared understanding. Advocacy and education are also important tools. Sharing personal stories and challenging negative stereotypes can help to change public perceptions and promote greater understanding. Furthermore, focusing on positive contributions to the community, such as volunteering or participating in civic activities, can help to counteract negative perceptions and demonstrate a commitment to responsible citizenship.

Remember, setbacks are a normal part of the re-entry process. Relationships may falter, social stigma may sting, and discouragement may creep in. It is during these times that the strength of one's support network is truly tested. Encouraging resilience, promoting self-compassion, and providing ongoing support are crucial for navigating these challenges. Remind individuals of their progress, celebrate their successes, and help them to maintain a sense of hope for the future.

Moreover, helping returning citizens learn about the concept of forgiveness can be an important step for their healing process. Some individuals may have hurt many people during the time that they were involved in criminal activity. It is important to teach them that apologizing can be a great way to start rebuilding the trust that they may have lost. Also, finding healthy hobbies and activities can aid in finding new connections.

In conclusion, family and social connections are vital to the successful re-entry of formerly incarcerated individuals. Rebuilding family relationships, developing healthy new connections, and navigating social stigma are complex challenges that require patience, empathy, and ongoing support. By fostering positive relationships and promoting social inclusion, we can help returning citizens to build stable, fulfilling lives and become contributing members of their communities. The ultimate goal is to create a society that embraces second chances and provides opportunities for all individuals to reach their full potential. I've witnessed firsthand the transformative power of these connections, and I remain committed to supporting the journey of returning citizens as they strive to rebuild their lives and reconnect with the world around them.

5.1 Rebuilding Family Relationships

Re-establishing family relationships after incarceration can feel like navigating a minefield, but it's a crucial step towards a fulfilling life. The time spent away creates distance, breeds misunderstandings, and often leaves deep scars on everyone involved. Understand that it's a process, not an event. It requires patience, commitment, and a willingness to confront uncomfortable truths, both yours and theirs. Before even initiating contact, take some time for honest self-reflection. Acknowledge the harm you've caused, not just to your immediate family, but potentially to extended family and the wider community. This isn't about wallowing in guilt, but about demonstrating genuine remorse and a commitment to making amends. Think specifically about the ways your actions have impacted each individual family member. Consider writing letters expressing your remorse, detailing how you plan to make amends, and asking for forgiveness. These letters shouldn't be demanding or manipulative, but sincere expressions of your regret.

The first contact after a long period of absence needs to be handled delicately. Don't assume you can simply pick up where you left off. Start small, maybe with a letter or a phone call, depending on what feels appropriate. Avoid overwhelming them with demands for immediate forgiveness or acceptance. Keep the initial conversations focused on listening. Ask about their lives, their challenges, and their successes. Show genuine interest in their well-being, even if it's painful to hear about a life that continued without you. Be prepared for a range of reactions, from cautious optimism to outright anger or rejection. Don't take it personally, even though it's hard not to. Understand that their reactions are a reflection of their own pain and trauma, not necessarily a judgment of you as a person. Give them space to process their feelings and respond in their own time. I have seen families who have had to cope with immense pain, often the financial, emotional and mental burden of supporting children, families and loved ones, and although it wasn't your intention to cause this pain, a sincere apology and willingness to listen is very important.

Building trust requires consistent effort and unwavering honesty. Avoid making promises you can't keep, especially in the early stages of reconnection. Small acts of reliability are more powerful than grand gestures. If you say you'll call, call. If you offer to help with something, follow through. Be transparent about your struggles and challenges, but avoid using them as excuses for your past behavior. Family members need to see that you're taking responsibility for your actions and actively working to change. Consider attending family therapy, either individually or as a group. A therapist can provide a neutral space for everyone to express their feelings, address unresolved conflicts, and develop healthier communication patterns. Family therapy can be particularly helpful in addressing the underlying issues that contributed to the breakdown of the relationship in the first place. Moreover, it can help family members develop empathy and understanding for each other's perspectives.

Establishing clear boundaries is essential for maintaining healthy relationships. This means respecting each other's limits and needs, even when they differ from your own. Don't pressure family members to do things they're not comfortable with, such as discussing sensitive topics or introducing you to their friends or colleagues. Be mindful of your own boundaries as well. Don't allow yourself to be manipulated or taken advantage of, even if you feel obligated to make amends. It's important to remember that reconciliation doesn't mean returning to the old dynamic. It's about creating a new relationship based on mutual respect, trust, and understanding. This may involve redefining roles and responsibilities within the family. For example, if you were previously a source of financial support, you may need to adjust your expectations and rely on your family for assistance while you get back on your feet. Conversely, if you were previously dependent on your family, you may need to take on more responsibility and contribute to the household.

Forgiveness is a critical component of rebuilding family relationships, but it's not always easy or immediate. Forgiveness is a process, not a one-time event. It requires time, patience, and a willingness to let go of resentment. You can't force someone to forgive you, but you can demonstrate genuine remorse and a commitment to change. Focus on your own actions and behaviors. Show your family members that you're worthy of their forgiveness. Even if they never fully forgive you, your efforts will not be in vain. The act of seeking forgiveness can be transformative, allowing you to heal from your past and move forward with greater self-awareness and compassion. Moreover, it can serve as a powerful example for other family members who may be struggling with forgiveness in their own lives.

There will be setbacks. Arguments will erupt, old wounds will re-open, and feelings of frustration and resentment will resurface. This is normal. Don't let these setbacks derail your progress. Instead, view them as opportunities to learn and grow. When conflict arises, try to remain calm and objective. Listen to your family members' perspectives without interrupting or becoming defensive. Validate their feelings, even if you don't agree with them. Seek common ground and work together to find solutions that meet everyone's needs. Remember that rebuilding family relationships is a marathon, not a sprint. It takes time, effort, and unwavering commitment. There will be moments of joy and connection, but also moments of pain and disappointment. The key is to stay focused on the long-term goal and to never give up hope. With patience, perseverance, and a genuine desire to make amends, you can rebuild trust, heal old wounds, and create a stronger, more fulfilling relationship with your family. I have seen people come back to families stronger and more loving than ever before.

5.2 Developing Healthy Relationships

Re-entering society after incarceration involves more than just finding a job and a place to live; it also necessitates rebuilding and forging healthy relationships. Many returning citizens face the daunting task of repairing fractured family bonds, navigating new social circles, and establishing trust with individuals who may harbor preconceived notions. This journey requires conscious effort, patience, and a willingness to learn new interpersonal skills. This chapter delves into the practical steps individuals can take to foster positive relationships and build a strong support network crucial for long-term success.

The foundation of any healthy relationship lies in effective communication. For individuals who have spent time in prison, adopting constructive communication styles might require unlearning ingrained patterns developed as coping mechanisms within that environment. Open and honest dialogue is paramount. It's about expressing your feelings and needs assertively, without resorting to aggression or defensiveness. Listen actively to others, demonstrating genuine interest in their perspectives, even when disagreements arise. Practicing "I" statements – such as "I feel frustrated when..." instead of "You always..." – can help de-escalate tense situations and promote understanding. Non-verbal communication is also crucial; maintain eye contact, use open body language, and be mindful of your tone of voice. Family members, for example, may need to unlearn past patterns of communication that led to conflict or distrust. If you struggle with communication, consider attending workshops or seeking guidance from a therapist or counselor specializing in interpersonal skills. They can provide tools and strategies to improve your ability to express yourself and connect with others.

Trust is another cornerstone of healthy relationships, and it can be particularly challenging to rebuild after periods of separation or due to past behaviors. Re-establishing trust takes time and consistent effort. It starts with demonstrating reliability and following through on your commitments, no matter how small they may seem. Be transparent and honest in your interactions, even when it's difficult. Acknowledge your past mistakes and take responsibility for your actions. Avoid making excuses or blaming others. Actively work to repair any damage you may have caused to relationships. For example, if you broke a promise to a family member, acknowledge the hurt you caused and commit to doing better in the future. Over time, consistent positive actions will gradually rebuild trust. Remember that rebuilding trust is a two-way street; be patient with others as they work to trust you again, and be willing to extend trust to them as well. If you have betrayed someone's trust in the past, a sincere apology and a commitment to changing your behavior are essential first steps.

Furthermore, setting and respecting boundaries is essential for maintaining healthy relationships. Clearly define your personal limits and communicate them to others. Boundaries can be physical, emotional, or mental. For instance, you might need to set a boundary with a family member who constantly criticizes you or invades your privacy. It's okay to say "no" to requests that make you uncomfortable or compromise your values. Boundaries protect your well-being and prevent others from taking advantage of you. Learning to assert your boundaries without feeling guilty or apologetic is crucial. Be firm but respectful when communicating your boundaries, and be prepared to enforce them if necessary. Healthy boundaries are not about controlling others; they are about protecting yourself and ensuring that your relationships are based on mutual respect and understanding. It is also crucial to be aware of other people's boundaries. Don't push them to do things they are uncomfortable with, and respect their decisions even if you don't agree with them.

Beyond family, building a supportive social network is vital for successful re-entry. This may involve reconnecting with old friends who offer positive influences or forging new relationships with individuals who share your values and goals. Seek out supportive communities or groups where you can connect with like-minded people, such as support groups for returning citizens, faith-based organizations, or community centers. Engaging in activities you enjoy can also be a great way to meet new people and build connections. Consider volunteering, joining a sports team, or taking a class. Building a social network provides a sense of belonging and reduces feelings of isolation, which can be a major challenge for individuals re-entering society. Be selective about the people you choose to associate with. Surround yourself with individuals who are positive, supportive, and encouraging. Avoid people who engage in negative behaviors or who undermine your efforts to change your life. It's essential to create a network of people who will support your goals and help you stay on track.

Finally, navigating social stigma can be a significant hurdle in developing healthy relationships. Many individuals who have been incarcerated face judgment and discrimination from others. Don't let the fear of judgment prevent you from building connections. Be open and honest about your past when you feel comfortable, but don't feel obligated to disclose your entire story to everyone you meet. Focus on your positive qualities and your commitment to change. Seek out individuals who are understanding and accepting, and avoid those who are judgmental or prejudiced. Remember that you are not defined by your past mistakes. You are a human being worthy of respect and compassion. Building healthy relationships is a process that takes time, patience, and effort. Don't get discouraged if you encounter setbacks along the way. Keep working on your communication skills, building trust, setting boundaries, and cultivating a supportive social network. With perseverance, you can create meaningful and fulfilling relationships that will enrich your life and support your journey toward responsible community re-entry. Seeking professional help from a therapist or counselor can provide valuable support and guidance in this process. Remember, developing healthy relationships is an investment in your future and a vital component of your overall well-being.

5.3 Navigating Social Stigma

The sting of judgment, the whispered words, the averted gaze – these are the realities many formerly incarcerated individuals face upon re-entering society. This social stigma, a deeply ingrained societal disapproval, acts as a powerful barrier, hindering their efforts to rebuild their lives and reintegrate into the community. Overcoming it requires a multi-faceted approach, demanding resilience from the individual and a willingness from society to embrace understanding and acceptance. We need to equip returning citizens with the tools to navigate these treacherous waters, while simultaneously challenging the prejudiced perceptions that fuel the stigma.

Let's be frank: acknowledging the source of the problem is vital. Social stigma stems from a complex interplay of fear, misunderstanding, and deeply rooted biases. The media often sensationalizes crime, perpetuating negative stereotypes and fueling public anxiety. Consequently, many people associate former inmates solely with their past offenses, overlooking their potential for rehabilitation and positive contributions. These assumptions, often unfounded, create a climate of distrust and exclusion, impacting every aspect of their lives, from finding employment and housing to forming meaningful relationships. It's a hurdle that seems insurmountable to many.

Building self-esteem is paramount. The experience of incarceration itself can be profoundly demoralizing, eroding self-worth and fostering feelings of shame and guilt. These feelings are often amplified by the stigma they encounter upon release. To combat this, individuals need to actively engage in activities that promote self-acceptance and positive self-image. This could involve setting achievable goals, focusing on personal strengths, and celebrating small victories. Participating in therapy or support groups can provide a safe space to process past experiences, address feelings of inadequacy, and develop coping mechanisms for dealing with negative self-talk. Remember, the journey towards self-acceptance is a marathon, not a sprint. It requires patience, perseverance, and a willingness to be kind to oneself.

Effective communication is key. One of the most challenging aspects of navigating social stigma is knowing how to respond to prejudiced comments or discriminatory treatment. Developing effective communication skills can empower individuals to confidently address these situations while protecting their emotional well-being. This involves learning how to assertively express their needs and boundaries, challenge negative stereotypes with factual information, and disengage from unproductive conversations. Practicing these skills through role-playing exercises or communication workshops can help build confidence and prepare them for real-world encounters. Furthermore, understanding their rights and legal protections can empower them to advocate for themselves and challenge discriminatory practices.

Seeking out supportive networks is crucial. Isolation can exacerbate the negative effects of social stigma, leading to feelings of loneliness, depression, and despair. Connecting with supportive individuals and groups can provide a sense of belonging, validation, and encouragement. This could involve joining support groups specifically for formerly incarcerated individuals, participating in community activities, or reconnecting with family members and friends who offer unconditional support. These networks provide a safe space to share experiences, receive guidance, and build resilience. It's a constant effort, but one that yields lasting reward.

Advocating for change is vital in dismantling societal prejudice. While individual efforts are essential, systemic change is needed to address the root causes of social stigma and create a more inclusive society. This involves advocating for policies that reduce barriers to re-entry, such as fair-chance hiring practices and access to affordable housing. It also requires challenging negative stereotypes in the media and promoting positive narratives about formerly incarcerated individuals. Engaging in public education campaigns, sharing personal stories, and supporting organizations that advocate for criminal justice reform can help raise awareness and shift public perceptions. This is not solely the responsibility of those who have been incarcerated; it requires the collective effort of community members, policymakers, and advocates.

Consider the power of storytelling. Sharing personal narratives can be a powerful tool for humanizing the experience of incarceration and challenging negative stereotypes. By sharing their stories, individuals can connect with others on a human level, fostering empathy and understanding. This could involve speaking at community events, writing articles or blog posts, or participating in documentaries or films. Sharing their experiences not only helps to break down barriers and challenge prejudices, but it can also empower others who are struggling with the stigma of incarceration.

Remember, patience is a virtue. Overcoming social stigma is a long and arduous process, requiring patience, perseverance, and unwavering self-belief. There will be setbacks and challenges along the way, but it's important to remain focused on the long-term goal of building a fulfilling and productive life. Celebrate small victories, learn from mistakes, and never give up on the belief that change is possible. Moreover, by consistently demonstrating responsible behavior and contributing positively to their communities, formerly incarcerated individuals can gradually erode negative perceptions and pave the way for a more inclusive and just society. It requires consistent effort.

6 Chapter 6: Legal and Ethical Considerations

Re-entering society after incarceration involves far more than just physical release; it demands a comprehensive understanding of the legal and ethical frameworks that govern one's life post-release. For those seeking to support returning citizens, a firm grasp of these considerations is paramount to facilitating responsible and sustainable reintegration. A misstep in either legal or ethical domains can have devastating consequences, jeopardizing not only the individual's freedom but also their ability to rebuild their lives and contribute positively to the community.

One of the primary hurdles for returning citizens lies in understanding their ongoing legal obligations. This encompasses everything from the specific conditions of parole or probation to any lingering restrictions imposed by the court. Parolees and probationers, for example, are typically subject to a range of conditions, such as regular reporting to a parole officer, restrictions on travel, prohibitions against associating with known criminals, and mandatory drug testing. Violation of any of these conditions, even seemingly minor ones, can result in immediate re-incarceration. It is essential that individuals clearly understand the parameters of their release and the potential consequences of non-compliance. This requires proactive engagement with parole officers, legal counsel, and support networks to ensure they are fully informed and equipped to meet their obligations. Moreover, supporting agencies should offer accessible resources and guidance, translating complex legal jargon into understandable terms. Beyond parole and probation, returning citizens may also face other legal challenges, such as outstanding warrants, child support obligations, or civil lawsuits. These issues can create significant barriers to securing employment, housing, and other essential services. Addressing these legal matters proactively is crucial for preventing further complications and fostering long-term stability. Providing access to legal aid services, pro bono attorneys, and community-based organizations that specialize in assisting returning citizens can make a significant difference in their ability to navigate these legal complexities.

Navigating the intricacies of parole and probation is often a minefield for those newly released. The conditions are often stringent, and the consequences for even minor infractions can be severe. It's not enough to simply know the rules; individuals must also understand the nuances of how these rules are enforced and how to effectively communicate with their parole or probation officers. Building a positive and transparent relationship with these officers is essential, as they often have considerable discretion in interpreting and enforcing the conditions of release. This involves being proactive in reporting any challenges or difficulties, demonstrating a genuine commitment to rehabilitation, and adhering strictly to the terms of their supervision. Additionally, understanding the appeals process and knowing their rights in the event of a violation are crucial for self-advocacy. Support organizations can play a vital role in providing guidance and advocacy during this process, ensuring that returning citizens are treated fairly and that their rights are protected. They can also help individuals develop coping mechanisms for dealing with the stress and anxiety associated with parole or probation supervision, reducing the likelihood of relapse or other behaviors that could lead to violations.

Ethical decision-making forms the bedrock of successful reintegration. It's about more than just avoiding illegal activities; it's about cultivating a sense of moral responsibility and making choices that align with societal values. For individuals who have spent time in prison, where a different set of norms and values may prevail, this can be a significant challenge. They may have developed survival strategies or coping mechanisms that, while necessary in prison, are not conducive to ethical behavior in the outside world. Therefore, ethical decision-making training should be an integral part of the re-entry process. This training should focus on identifying ethical dilemmas, analyzing potential consequences, and developing strategies for making responsible choices. It should also address issues such as honesty, integrity, respect for others, and accountability for one's actions. Furthermore, creating opportunities for returning citizens to engage in positive social activities and build relationships with ethical role models can reinforce these values and provide a sense of belonging and purpose. This can involve volunteering, participating in community service projects, or joining support groups that promote ethical behavior.

Acknowledging the impact of crime on victims is an often-overlooked but crucial aspect of responsible re-entry. A deep understanding of victimology fosters empathy and promotes a sense of accountability. It is essential that returning citizens grasp the far-reaching consequences of their actions, not only for the direct victims but also for their families, friends, and the wider community. Victim awareness programs can provide valuable insights into the emotional, psychological, and financial toll that crime takes on individuals and communities. These programs can also help returning citizens develop a sense of remorse and a desire to make amends for their past actions. It's important to emphasize that victim awareness is not about self-flagellation or dwelling on past mistakes, but rather about learning from those mistakes and using them as a catalyst for positive change. It's about developing a genuine understanding of the harm caused and committing to behaviors that prevent future harm.

Restorative justice offers a powerful framework for addressing the harm caused by crime and promoting healing for both offenders and victims. This approach emphasizes repairing the harm caused by crime, rather than simply punishing the offender. Restorative justice practices can include victim-offender mediation, community conferencing, and restitution programs. These processes provide opportunities for victims to share their experiences, express their needs, and participate in determining how the harm can be repaired. They also provide offenders with the chance to take responsibility for their actions, make amends for the harm they have caused, and reintegrate into the community in a meaningful way. Restorative justice is not a replacement for traditional criminal justice processes, but rather a complementary approach that can address the underlying causes of crime and promote healing and reconciliation. Implementing restorative justice principles requires a collaborative effort between criminal justice professionals, community organizations, and victims' advocates. It also requires a shift in mindset, from a focus on punishment to a focus on restoration and healing. When implemented effectively, restorative justice can contribute to safer communities, reduced recidivism rates, and a greater sense of justice for all.

6.1 Understanding Legal Obligations

The legal landscape that confronts individuals re-entering society after incarceration is a complex web of federal, state, and local laws, regulations, and conditions. Understanding these obligations is paramount to avoiding recidivism and achieving true reintegration. Many individuals leave prison with limited understanding of their rights and responsibilities, setting them up for potential violations and setbacks. One of the first steps toward successful re-entry is acquiring comprehensive knowledge of these legal obligations.

Navigating parole or probation, a common component of re-entry, involves strict adherence to specific conditions set by the court or parole board. These conditions can vary widely, but often include regular reporting to a supervising officer, maintaining employment, abstaining from drug and alcohol use, refraining from contact with certain individuals (often co-conspirators or victims), and adhering to curfew restrictions. The specifics of these conditions must be clear to the individual, because ignorance is not a valid excuse for non-compliance. It is critical that parolees and probationers receive a detailed explanation of their conditions, preferably in writing, and have opportunities to ask questions and seek clarification. This explanation should come from the supervising officer, but also from legal aid organizations, or re-entry programs.

Beyond parole and probation, individuals face numerous other legal obligations that are often overlooked. These can include restrictions on voting rights, which vary by state; understanding these restrictions is a civic duty and a cornerstone of societal re-entry. Depending on the nature of the offense, there may be limitations on employment opportunities, particularly in fields requiring background checks or security clearances. Some professions, such as law enforcement, healthcare, and childcare, may be permanently barred to individuals with certain convictions. Awareness of these limitations is crucial for realistic career planning and avoiding wasted time and resources pursuing unattainable goals.

Another area of legal obligation involves registering as a sex offender, if applicable. These laws carry strict requirements, including periodic in-person registration, notification of address changes, and limitations on where registered offenders can live or work. Failure to comply with these requirements can result in severe penalties, including re-incarceration. The complexities of sex offender registration laws are well-documented, and often differ significantly from state to state. Re-entering citizens must get precise legal advice.

Financial obligations also demand scrutiny. Many formerly incarcerated individuals face significant debt, including court fees, fines, restitution to victims, and child support arrears. Ignoring these obligations can lead to wage garnishment, seizure of assets, and further legal complications. Creating a realistic budget and prioritizing debt repayment are essential steps toward financial stability. Resources such as credit counseling services and financial literacy programs can provide valuable assistance in managing finances and navigating debt repayment options.

Moreover, understanding housing laws is crucial. Discrimination based on prior criminal history is often illegal, but landlords may still be hesitant to rent to individuals with a criminal record. Familiarizing oneself with fair housing laws and knowing one's rights as a tenant is paramount. Additionally, individuals should be aware of any local ordinances that may restrict where they can live, especially if they are subject to parole or probation conditions.

There are also crucial differences between states' laws. Individuals should understand their rights and responsibilities in their specific location. Laws regarding expungement and sealing of criminal records vary widely, and pursuing these options can significantly improve employment and housing prospects. Expungement essentially erases a criminal record, while sealing makes it inaccessible to most employers and landlords. Eligibility for expungement or sealing depends on the nature of the offense, the length of time since the conviction, and other factors. Consulting with an attorney or legal aid organization can help determine eligibility and navigate the expungement process.

It's also important to consider the potential for civil lawsuits. If someone's actions, even if they did not lead to a criminal conviction, caused harm to another person, they could still be sued in civil court. This could lead to financial judgments against them, further complicating their re-entry process. Understanding personal liability and taking steps to protect oneself from potential lawsuits is essential.

Further, victim notification laws are crucial, specifically in cases of violent crime. The victim might need to be informed when the inmate is released, which could trigger complex emotions and potentially lead to safety concerns for both parties. Programs that facilitate communication and reconciliation between offenders and victims, when appropriate and desired by the victim, can contribute to healing and restorative justice.

Ethical considerations are also intertwined with legal obligations. While the law sets minimum standards of conduct, ethical behavior goes beyond mere compliance. Making ethical choices, such as being honest with employers and family members, taking responsibility for past actions, and contributing to the community, can build trust and foster positive relationships.

Accessing legal resources is essential. Legal aid organizations, pro bono attorneys, and re-entry programs often provide free or low-cost legal assistance to formerly incarcerated individuals. These resources can help navigate complex legal issues, understand rights and responsibilities, and advocate for fair treatment. Building relationships with legal professionals can be invaluable in preventing legal problems and resolving disputes.

In conclusion, understanding legal obligations is a fundamental aspect of successful re-entry. By acquiring knowledge of parole and probation conditions, employment restrictions, sex offender registration requirements, financial obligations, housing laws, and other legal issues, individuals can avoid pitfalls and build a foundation for a law-abiding and productive life. Accessing legal resources and making ethical choices further enhance the chances of successful reintegration into society. Legal information is empowering.

6.2 Navigating Parole and Probation

Stepping out of prison and into the arms of parole or probation can feel like walking a tightrope. On one side, the freedom to rebuild your life; on the other, the ever-present threat of falling back into incarceration. This chapter is designed to help you navigate that tightrope with confidence and understanding. Parole and probation, while often used interchangeably, are distinct forms of community supervision. Parole is granted by a parole board after a period of imprisonment, while probation is typically imposed by a judge as an alternative to incarceration, or sometimes, a period of probation follows a shorter jail sentence. Both involve adhering to specific conditions and reporting to a supervising officer. These conditions can range from maintaining employment and abstaining from drug and alcohol use to restrictions on travel and association with certain individuals. Understanding the nuances of your specific situation is paramount.

The first step to successfully navigating parole or probation is to fully grasp the conditions imposed upon you. Don't rely on second-hand information or assumptions. Your supervising officer is your primary resource. Request a detailed written explanation of each condition, and don't hesitate to ask for clarification if anything is unclear. Ignorance is not an excuse. For example, a condition might state "no contact with known felons." What constitutes "contact?" Does a chance encounter at a grocery store violate the condition? It's your responsibility to seek clarity and avoid unintentional violations. Understanding the geography of your restrictions is crucial as well. Some conditions may limit travel outside of a specific county or state without prior approval. Violating these geographical boundaries, even unknowingly, can have serious consequences. Furthermore, be meticulously organized in maintaining records of your compliance. Keep copies of employment verification, attendance records for required programs, and any other documentation that demonstrates your commitment to fulfilling the conditions of your supervision.

Building a positive relationship with your supervising officer is also important. While they are responsible for monitoring your compliance, they can also be a source of support and guidance. Treat them with respect, be honest and forthcoming, and promptly report any challenges you encounter. Transparency is key. If you are struggling to find employment or experiencing difficulty with a specific condition, communicate this to your officer. They may be able to connect you with resources or make recommendations to the court or parole board to modify the conditions of your supervision. Remember, your supervising officer has a caseload of other individuals, and proactive communication demonstrates responsibility and a genuine desire to succeed. Showing that you are taking ownership of your re-entry process can foster a more collaborative and supportive relationship. Remember, your officer is not necessarily your friend, however. They are in charge of monitoring you and will use everything you say against you if you are in violation of your release terms. Be careful about what you say and maintain respect.

Moreover, developing a strong support system outside of the supervision structure is vital for long-term success. Family, friends, mentors, and community organizations can provide emotional support, practical assistance, and a sense of belonging. Isolation can be a significant risk factor for recidivism, so actively seek out positive and supportive relationships. Consider joining a support group for individuals in re-entry or connecting with a faith-based organization that offers assistance to formerly incarcerated individuals. These groups can provide a safe space to share your experiences, learn from others, and build a network of support. Furthermore, actively engage in activities that promote your well-being and personal growth. This could include pursuing educational opportunities, volunteering in your community, or engaging in hobbies that bring you joy and fulfillment. By focusing on your personal development, you can build self-esteem, reduce stress, and create a more positive and productive life.

Navigating drug testing, a common condition of parole and probation, requires a proactive and responsible approach. Understand the specific protocols for testing, including the frequency, location, and type of test administered. If you have a legitimate medical condition that requires medication, inform your supervising officer and provide documentation from your doctor. Avoid any substances that could trigger a false positive, such as certain over-the-counter medications or herbal remedies. If you struggle with substance abuse, seek professional help immediately. Many programs offer specialized treatment for individuals in re-entry, and your supervising officer can provide referrals. Honesty about your struggles is crucial, and seeking help demonstrates a commitment to your recovery. Furthermore, be aware of the consequences of failing a drug test. This could result in increased supervision, mandatory treatment, or even revocation of your parole or probation. Taking responsibility for your actions and seeking help when needed is essential for maintaining your freedom. Finally, remember that parole and probation are not permanent. If you successfully complete your period of supervision, you will be released from all conditions and obligations. However, even after completing your supervision, you may still face challenges related to your criminal record. Explore options for expungement or sealing your record, which can remove barriers to employment, housing, and other opportunities. Contact a legal aid organization or attorney to learn about the eligibility requirements and application process in your state. Furthermore, continue to build upon the positive changes you have made during your supervision. Maintain your support system, engage in activities that promote your well-being, and strive to be a contributing member of your community. Successful re-entry is a journey, not a destination, and continued effort is essential for long-term success. With perseverance, accountability, and a strong support system, you can successfully navigate the challenges of parole and probation and build a brighter future for yourself and your community. This chapter has laid the foundation for you to understand the path ahead.

6.3 Ethical Decision-Making

Ethical dilemmas are inescapable realities for individuals re-entering society after incarceration. Life after release presents a maze of choices, where the lines between right and wrong can blur under the pressure of survival, societal expectations, and the enduring impact of past experiences. Understanding the nuances of ethical decision-making, therefore, becomes a critical skill for navigating this complex terrain and building a foundation for responsible community reintegration.

The first step involves cultivating a robust sense of self-awareness. This entails honestly confronting past actions, acknowledging the harm caused, and taking responsibility for one's role in those events. It's not about wallowing in guilt, but rather about understanding the factors that contributed to unethical choices in the past. Were these choices driven by desperation, peer pressure, a lack of understanding of the consequences, or a combination of factors? Identifying these patterns allows individuals to proactively address potential triggers and develop alternative coping mechanisms. For instance, someone who previously engaged in theft due to financial hardship might explore job training programs or budgeting skills workshops to address this underlying vulnerability upon release. Knowing yourself requires identifying your values, the principles that will guide your decisions. Understanding what is truly important allows you to align your choices with your core beliefs.

Beyond self-reflection, consider the ethical frameworks that can provide guidance in challenging situations. Utilitarianism, for example, focuses on choosing the action that produces the greatest good for the greatest number of people. While seemingly straightforward, applying this principle in real-world scenarios can be difficult. How do you weigh the potential benefits for one group against the potential harm to another? Deontology, on the other hand, emphasizes adherence to moral rules and duties, regardless of the consequences. For instance, a deontological approach might dictate that lying is always wrong, even if it seems like it would lead to a positive outcome in a particular situation. Virtue ethics focuses on developing good character traits, such as honesty, integrity, and compassion. By cultivating these virtues, individuals are more likely to make ethical choices intuitively. While no single framework provides a perfect solution to every ethical dilemma, understanding these different perspectives can broaden your horizons and provide valuable insights.

Another crucial aspect of ethical decision-making involves considering the potential consequences of your actions. This requires a careful analysis of the various stakeholders involved and the impact that your choices could have on them. Who will benefit from your decision? Who might be harmed? What are the short-term and long-term consequences? It's essential to consider not only the immediate, obvious consequences but also the ripple effects that your actions could create. For instance, accepting a job that requires you to misrepresent your past might seem like a quick fix to secure employment, but it could ultimately lead to more significant problems down the road if the truth is revealed. It also involves understanding the legal ramifications of various choices. Even if an action seems morally justifiable, it could still be illegal and lead to further legal complications, hindering your progress toward successful re-entry. Understanding parole and probation restrictions is vital to make ethical choices.

However, ethical decision-making is rarely a solitary endeavor. Seeking advice and guidance from trusted mentors, counselors, or members of your support network can provide valuable perspective and help you to avoid making impulsive or ill-considered choices. These individuals can serve as sounding boards, helping you to think through the potential consequences of your actions and identify any blind spots in your reasoning. They can also provide emotional support and encouragement when you are facing difficult ethical dilemmas. This is especially important when dealing with social stigma and the temptation to hide past wrong-doings. Being open about the past, when and where appropriate, is important to make ethical choices.

Remember, ethical decision-making is not about achieving perfection. It's about making a sincere effort to do the right thing, even when it's difficult or unpopular. It's about learning from your mistakes and striving to make better choices in the future. This journey involves continuously refining your understanding of ethical principles, seeking guidance from trusted sources, and reflecting on the consequences of your actions. Develop a support network that encourages ethical behavior and provides accountability. Engage with individuals who share your values and are committed to responsible community re-entry.

It is easy to fall when you have been convicted for an offence, and community members may not be very supportive. However, the key is to understand the importance of taking the right choices, to show the community that you have changed. It is easier to build a good name, than repair a bad one.

Navigating the complexities of life after incarceration demands a commitment to ethical principles. By cultivating self-awareness, understanding ethical frameworks, considering the consequences of your actions, seeking guidance from trusted sources, and embracing continuous learning, you can navigate the ethical dilemmas that arise and build a foundation for responsible community reintegration. This commitment to ethical conduct not only benefits you personally but also contributes to a more just and equitable society. Ultimately, responsible re-entry is not just about avoiding recidivism; it's about becoming a contributing member of society who lives with integrity and makes choices that promote the well-being of others.

6.4 Victim Awareness

Acknowledging the harm caused is a pivotal step in the rehabilitation process, and for those re-entering society after incarceration, a sincere understanding of victim awareness is paramount. It's not simply a legal requirement, but a fundamental shift in perspective that can pave the way for true accountability and personal growth. We're talking about fostering genuine empathy for the individuals and communities affected by crime.

The journey starts with education. Many incarcerated individuals haven't had the opportunity to truly consider the ripple effects of their actions. Providing comprehensive victim impact statements, not just from the legal perspective but through personal narratives and facilitated discussions, can be profoundly impactful. These sessions should not be designed as guilt trips, but rather as opportunities to connect with the human cost of crime. This necessitates creating a safe and supportive environment where inmates feel comfortable exploring their emotions and confronting the consequences of their behavior. It's about helping them understand that their actions didn't exist in a vacuum; they had real and lasting repercussions on real people.

However, victim awareness isn't a passive exercise. It requires active engagement and a willingness to confront uncomfortable truths. This can involve restorative justice practices, where appropriate and with the consent of the victim. Restorative justice offers a structured process for offenders to take responsibility for their actions, make amends to the victim (where the victim is willing), and reintegrate into the community. It's important to emphasize that restorative justice is not a way to "get off easy," but rather a challenging and demanding process that requires genuine remorse and a commitment to making amends. Even in cases where direct contact with the victim is not possible or desired, alternative forms of restorative justice can be implemented, such as community service that directly benefits victims of crime or participation in victim empathy programs.

And what does true empathy entail? It's more than just feeling sorry. It's about understanding the victim's perspective, acknowledging their pain, and recognizing the long-term impact of the crime on their life. This requires developing active listening skills and the ability to put oneself in another's shoes. This is especially crucial because many re-entering citizens may have experienced trauma themselves, making it harder to connect with others. The focus here is to create empathy and compassion through structured exercises and cognitive behavioral therapy.

Accountability is another vital component. It's not enough to simply acknowledge the harm caused; offenders must take responsibility for their actions and make a commitment to preventing future harm. This can involve developing a personalized re-entry plan that addresses the underlying factors that contributed to their criminal behavior, such as substance abuse, anger management issues, or lack of job skills. It also means understanding the legal consequences of their actions and adhering to the conditions of their parole or probation. It may also require financial restitution to the victim and this is where financial literacy can be helpful in understanding how the offenders are managing the payments.

Beyond individual accountability, it's important to foster a sense of community responsibility. Re-entering citizens need to understand that they are not just responsible for their own actions, but also for contributing to a safer and more just society. This can involve participating in community service projects, mentoring at-risk youth, or advocating for policies that support crime prevention and rehabilitation. By becoming active members of their communities, re-entering citizens can demonstrate their commitment to making amends and preventing future harm.

It is important to recognize that victim awareness is not a one-size-fits-all approach. Each individual's journey is unique, and the specific strategies used to foster victim awareness must be tailored to their individual needs and circumstances. Factors such as the nature of the crime, the offender's background, and the victim's preferences should all be taken into consideration.

Finally, sustaining a commitment to victim awareness requires ongoing support and reinforcement. Re-entering citizens need to have access to resources and services that can help them maintain their progress and avoid relapse. This can include continued therapy, support groups, and mentoring programs. It also means creating a supportive community that encourages accountability and provides opportunities for personal growth. Remember, this shift requires continuous nurturing and reinforcement. It's not a checkbox to be ticked off, but a lifelong commitment to ethical behavior and social responsibility. By prioritizing victim awareness, we can create a pathway towards genuine rehabilitation, promoting safer communities and a more just society for everyone.

6.5 Restorative Justice Principles

Restorative justice offers a powerful alternative to traditional punitive measures, especially as individuals prepare for re-entry into society. It shifts the focus from punishment to repairing the harm caused by crime, emphasizing accountability, healing, and community involvement. For those leaving incarceration, engaging with restorative justice principles can be transformative, fostering a sense of responsibility and facilitating a smoother reintegration process. It is a chance to acknowledge their actions, address the harm caused, and begin to repair relationships with those affected.

At its core, restorative justice revolves around three key questions: Who has been harmed? What are their needs? And whose obligation is it to meet those needs? These questions guide the process, ensuring that the focus remains on the victims of crime and their healing. Unlike the adversarial nature of the traditional legal system, restorative justice seeks to create a collaborative environment where all parties can participate in finding solutions. This involvement can empower victims, giving them a voice in the justice process and allowing them to express their needs and concerns directly to the offender. This is a significant departure from the feeling of powerlessness that many victims experience within the traditional legal framework.

One of the primary benefits of restorative justice for inmates preparing for re-entry is the opportunity for accountability. It encourages individuals to take responsibility for their actions and understand the impact they have had on others. This can be a challenging process, but it is essential for fostering genuine remorse and a commitment to making amends. Instead of simply serving a sentence, individuals are actively involved in addressing the harm they have caused, developing empathy, and recognizing the human cost of their actions. This process can lead to a deeper understanding of the consequences of their choices and a stronger desire to live a law-abiding life. Furthermore, restorative justice provides a platform for offenders to express remorse and offer apologies, which can be incredibly meaningful for victims.

Victim empowerment is another crucial aspect of restorative justice. It gives victims a voice in the justice process, allowing them to share their experiences, express their needs, and participate in the development of a restorative plan. This can be incredibly healing, helping victims to feel heard, validated, and respected. It also allows them to regain a sense of control over their lives after experiencing the trauma of crime. For many victims, simply having the opportunity to confront the offender and ask questions can be incredibly empowering, providing a sense of closure and enabling them to move forward.

Restorative justice processes often involve facilitated dialogues between offenders, victims, and community members. These dialogues create a safe space for open communication, allowing all parties to share their perspectives and work together to develop a restorative plan. The plan might include restitution, community service, or other actions that address the harm caused by the crime. It is important to note that participation in restorative justice is always voluntary, and all parties must feel safe and comfortable engaging in the process.

For inmates preparing for re-entry, participation in restorative justice programs can be a valuable asset. It demonstrates a commitment to accountability, remorse, and making amends, which can be viewed favorably by parole boards and potential employers. It also provides an opportunity to develop empathy, communication skills, and problem-solving abilities, all of which are essential for successful reintegration into society. Moreover, restorative justice can help to repair damaged relationships with family members and other members of the community, which can provide a crucial support system upon release.

Implementing restorative justice within correctional facilities requires a commitment to training and education for both inmates and staff. It is essential to create a culture of understanding and support for restorative principles, ensuring that all parties are aware of the benefits and limitations of the process. Correctional staff need to be trained in facilitation techniques, conflict resolution, and trauma-informed practices to effectively guide restorative justice dialogues. Inmates need to be educated about the principles of restorative justice, the importance of accountability, and the benefits of participating in the process.

However, the success of restorative justice hinges on careful implementation and a nuanced understanding of its limitations. It is not a one-size-fits-all solution and may not be appropriate in all cases. It is crucial to assess the needs and preferences of victims, ensuring that they are comfortable with the process and that their safety is paramount. In some cases, victims may not be willing or able to participate in restorative justice, and their wishes must be respected.

Furthermore, restorative justice should not be seen as a substitute for traditional legal processes. It is often used in conjunction with the traditional justice system, providing an opportunity for healing and reconciliation alongside accountability and punishment. It is important to ensure that offenders are held accountable for their actions and that victims receive the support and resources they need to heal and rebuild their lives.

Ultimately, restorative justice offers a path towards healing, accountability, and community reconciliation. By focusing on repairing the harm caused by crime, it empowers victims, holds offenders accountable, and fosters a sense of community responsibility. For inmates preparing for re-entry, engaging with restorative justice principles can be a transformative experience, providing an opportunity to make amends, develop empathy, and build a foundation for a more responsible and fulfilling life. Embracing this approach requires a paradigm shift from a punitive mindset to one that prioritizes healing, restoration, and the creation of a safer and more just society for all.

7 Chapter 7: Community Integration and Support

Finding your footing after incarceration hinges significantly on the stability of your living situation, and it's often the first and most critical hurdle. Securing safe, affordable housing is paramount; without a place to call your own, the challenges of finding work, maintaining sobriety, and rebuilding relationships are exponentially amplified. Start by connecting with local organizations specializing in housing assistance for returning citizens. These groups often maintain lists of landlords willing to rent to individuals with criminal records, and they can guide you through the application process, which often involves addressing concerns about your past. Transitional housing programs can provide a temporary, structured environment, offering support services such as case management, job training, and counseling. Remember to be upfront and honest with potential landlords about your history; transparency can build trust and demonstrate your commitment to a fresh start. Don't be discouraged by initial rejections, persistence is key.

Next, a network of community resources can be a lifeline in your re-entry journey. Consider the services available at local community centers, faith-based organizations, and non-profit agencies. These entities often provide a spectrum of support, including food banks, clothing assistance, transportation vouchers, and legal aid. Many offer specialized programs tailored to the needs of formerly incarcerated individuals, such as mentoring, job placement assistance, and substance abuse counseling. Reach out to these organizations early in your re-entry process to establish connections and learn about the resources available in your area. Building relationships with community leaders and volunteers can also provide invaluable support and guidance. Don't hesitate to ask for help; it's a sign of strength, not weakness.

Moreover, empowering yourself through advocacy is critical for long-term success. Understand your rights and responsibilities as a returning citizen, and learn how to advocate for yourself in various situations. This includes knowing your rights regarding employment, housing, and access to services. Participate in community forums and meetings to voice your concerns and advocate for policies that support successful re-entry. Share your story with others to raise awareness about the challenges faced by formerly incarcerated individuals and to inspire hope and change. Joining advocacy groups or becoming a peer mentor can provide opportunities to advocate for yourself and others, while also building a supportive network. Remember, your voice matters, and your experience can be a powerful tool for creating positive change.

Beyond these initial steps, consider the longer-term strategies for sustained community integration. Actively participate in community events and activities to build social connections and foster a sense of belonging. Volunteer your time to local causes to give back to the community and demonstrate your commitment to positive change. Seek out opportunities for continued learning and skill development to enhance your employability and personal growth. Cultivate healthy relationships with family, friends, and mentors to provide ongoing support and encouragement. Finally, remember that re-entry is a process, not an event, and setbacks are inevitable. Be patient with yourself, celebrate your successes, and learn from your challenges.

Furthermore, accessing the right resources involves a nuanced understanding of what's available and how to navigate the system. Many communities offer comprehensive re-entry resource guides, often available online or through local social service agencies. These guides provide detailed information about various programs, eligibility requirements, and contact information. When seeking assistance, be prepared to provide documentation such as your identification, release papers, and proof of address. Be persistent in your efforts, as navigating bureaucratic systems can be challenging. Don't be afraid to ask for clarification or assistance from case managers or other professionals who can help you navigate the process. Consider attending workshops or training sessions on topics such as resume writing, job interviewing, and financial management to improve your chances of success.

In addition, building bridges with the community requires proactive engagement and a willingness to connect with others. Attend community events, join local clubs or organizations, and participate in volunteer activities to meet new people and build relationships. Be open and honest about your past, but focus on your present and future goals. Demonstrate your commitment to responsible citizenship by following the law, paying your taxes, and contributing to the community in positive ways. Seek out opportunities to mentor or support others who are going through similar challenges. Remember, building trust and acceptance takes time, but it is essential for long-term integration.

Finally, sustaining long-term success requires a holistic approach that addresses all aspects of your life. Prioritize your physical and mental health by eating a healthy diet, exercising regularly, and seeking professional help when needed. Develop healthy coping mechanisms for managing stress and avoiding relapse. Set realistic goals and celebrate your achievements along the way. Surround yourself with supportive people who believe in you and encourage you to stay on track. Remember that you are not alone in this journey, and there are people who care about you and want to see you succeed. With determination, resilience, and the right support, you can build a brighter future for yourself and your community.

It's worth reiterating, persistence is key. The road to successful reentry is often fraught with obstacles, but remember that setbacks are temporary and do not define your potential. Stay focused on your goals, learn from your mistakes, and never give up on yourself. With the right support and a commitment to positive change, you can overcome any challenge and achieve your dreams.

7.1 Finding Housing and Shelter

The hunt for stable housing after release can feel like navigating a minefield, especially when you're just trying to get your feet back on the ground. Remember this: securing safe and affordable housing is often the single most important factor in preventing homelessness and promoting long-term stability. Without a safe place to call home, it's incredibly difficult to find a job, maintain your health, and reconnect with your family. It's the foundation upon which you rebuild your life.

Understand your eligibility for public housing programs. Many returning citizens are eligible for subsidized housing assistance, such as Section 8 vouchers or public housing units. However, the application process can be lengthy and complicated, and waiting lists are often extensive. Don't get discouraged by the wait; start the application process as soon as possible, even before your release. Gather all necessary documentation, like identification, proof of income (if you have any), and any relevant court documents. Investigate local housing authorities and their specific requirements; some might have restrictions based on your offense, but there are often exceptions and waivers available. Be upfront and honest about your past; transparency is often appreciated and can help build trust with housing providers. Also, remember that some housing programs may have restrictions on who can live with you, so clarify those details early on to avoid future complications.

Explore transitional housing options. These facilities provide temporary housing and supportive services specifically designed for individuals re-entering the community after incarceration. Unlike emergency shelters, transitional housing offers a more structured environment with case management, job training, and counseling services. Seek out programs that align with your specific needs and goals. Some programs focus on substance abuse recovery, while others specialize in vocational training or family reunification. Be prepared to follow program rules and expectations, which may include curfews, drug testing, and participation in group activities. The length of stay in transitional housing typically ranges from a few months to two years, giving you valuable time to stabilize your life and develop a long-term housing plan. Remember that transitional housing is a stepping stone, not a permanent solution, so actively work towards securing independent housing during your stay.

Consider halfway houses. These are similar to transitional housing but often provide a more structured environment with stricter rules and supervision. Halfway houses are typically operated by correctional agencies or non-profit organizations and are designed to help individuals gradually transition back into society. If you're on parole or probation, your supervising officer may recommend or require you to live in a halfway house as a condition of your release. While halfway houses can provide a safe and supportive environment, they can also feel restrictive. Be prepared to adhere to strict rules and regulations, including curfews, visitation policies, and restrictions on personal belongings. Participate actively in program activities and counseling sessions to maximize the benefits of your stay. Remember that halfway houses are designed to help you develop the skills and behaviors necessary for successful re-entry, so embrace the opportunity to learn and grow.

Don't overlook sober living homes. If you're struggling with substance abuse, sober living homes can provide a safe and supportive environment to maintain your sobriety and rebuild your life. These homes offer a structured environment with regular drug testing, house meetings, and peer support. Sober living homes are often privately owned and operated, so the cost can vary depending on the location and amenities. Look for homes that are certified or accredited by reputable organizations to ensure quality and safety. Be prepared to follow house rules and participate actively in recovery activities. Sober living homes can be an invaluable resource for individuals committed to long-term sobriety, providing a supportive community and a safe place to live.

Reach out to local non-profit organizations. Many non-profits offer housing assistance and supportive services to returning citizens. These organizations can help you navigate the complex housing system, connect you with available resources, and provide financial assistance for rent and security deposits. Research local organizations that specialize in re-entry services and schedule an appointment to discuss your housing needs. Be prepared to provide documentation of your past incarceration and any other relevant information. Nonprofits can also connect you with other essential services, such as job training, mental health counseling, and legal assistance. These organizations are often a lifeline for returning citizens, providing a sense of hope and support during a challenging time.

Explore shared housing options. Renting a room in a shared house or apartment can be a more affordable option than renting an entire unit on your own. Look for roommate matching services or online platforms that connect individuals seeking shared housing. Be upfront and honest about your past with potential roommates; transparency can help build trust and avoid misunderstandings. Establish clear expectations and boundaries regarding rent, utilities, and household responsibilities. Shared housing can provide a sense of community and support, but it's important to find roommates who are respectful and compatible with your lifestyle.

Consider alternative housing options. If traditional housing options are not available, consider alternative solutions such as micro-housing, co-living spaces, or temporary housing in a motel or campground. These options may not be ideal for the long term, but they can provide a temporary solution while you search for more permanent housing. Research the safety and suitability of these options before committing to them. Be aware of any restrictions or regulations that may apply, such as limits on the length of stay or requirements for background checks. While alternative housing options may not be ideal, they can provide a safe and secure place to stay while you navigate the challenges of re-entry.

Remember that persistence is key. Finding housing after incarceration can be a long and challenging process. Don't get discouraged by setbacks or rejections. Keep applying for housing programs, reaching

out to organizations, and exploring different options. Be proactive and persistent in your search, and don't be afraid to ask for help. With determination and support, you can find safe and stable housing and build a successful life after incarceration. Your resilience is your greatest asset; never give up on yourself.
Prioritize Safety. Ensure the housing you consider is located in a safe neighborhood with access to essential services like public transportation, grocery stores, and healthcare facilities. Research crime rates in the area and consider whether the environment will be conducive to your rehabilitation. A supportive and safe environment is essential for your well-being and your ability to successfully re-enter the community.

7.2 Community Resources and Services

Stepping out of the prison gates is just the first step; truly re-entering society means navigating a complex web of community resources and services. These often-overlooked lifelines can be the difference between successful reintegration and a return to old patterns. Securing stable housing, accessing healthcare, finding employment assistance – these are all critical components of a successful transition, and they rarely happen in isolation. I have found that a proactive approach, even before release, makes all the difference.
Understanding the local landscape is key. Begin by researching organizations in your target community while you are still incarcerated. Many states and counties have dedicated re-entry programs listed on their government websites. These programs often provide comprehensive services, including case management, housing assistance, job training, and mental health support. Don't underestimate the power of a simple Google search using terms like "re-entry services [your

city/county]" or "community resources for formerly incarcerated individuals [your state]". Public libraries can be invaluable resources as well, offering not only internet access and databases but also librarians who can help navigate local services. Furthermore, consider reaching out to faith-based organizations. Churches, synagogues, mosques, and other religious institutions often have outreach programs that provide food, clothing, shelter, and spiritual guidance. These can be especially helpful in building a supportive community. Navigating the maze of housing options is often one of the most immediate and daunting challenges. Stable housing is foundational to successful re-entry; without it, securing employment, maintaining sobriety, and staying connected to services becomes exponentially harder. Begin by exploring transitional housing programs specifically designed for formerly incarcerated individuals. These programs provide temporary housing, often with supportive services like case management, substance abuse counseling, and job readiness training. Many non-profit organizations offer such programs, and eligibility requirements vary. It's also essential to understand your rights as a tenant. Landlords cannot discriminate against you based solely on your criminal record in many jurisdictions, although they can consider factors like safety concerns and previous evictions. Familiarize yourself with local fair housing laws and seek legal assistance if you believe you have been discriminated against. Section 8 vouchers, if you are eligible, can provide significant rental assistance, but the application process can be lengthy, so it's wise to start early. Exploring shared living arrangements with roommates can be a more affordable option, although it requires careful consideration of compatibility and personal boundaries.

Securing employment is another cornerstone of successful re-entry, and various resources can help you gain a foothold in the job market. Start by assessing your skills and identifying potential career paths. Community colleges and vocational schools offer a range of training programs that can equip you with the skills employers are looking for. Many organizations specialize in providing job training and placement services for formerly incarcerated individuals, offering assistance with resume writing, interview skills, and job searching. Consider apprenticeship programs, which provide on-the-job training and a pathway to skilled trades. Don't overlook the power of networking. Connect with friends, family, and former colleagues who may be able to provide leads or introductions. Attend job fairs and community events to meet potential employers. Be honest about your background during the hiring process, but focus on your strengths, skills, and willingness to learn. Many employers are increasingly open to hiring individuals with criminal records, recognizing the value of second chances.

Addressing healthcare needs, both physical and mental, is crucial for overall well-being and successful re-entry. Many formerly incarcerated individuals have unmet healthcare needs due to limited access to care while incarcerated. Upon release, it's essential to establish a relationship with a primary care physician and access any necessary specialist care. Medicaid and other government-funded programs can provide affordable healthcare coverage for eligible individuals. Community health centers offer a range of services, often on a sliding fee scale, making them accessible to low-income individuals. Mental health services are particularly critical, as many formerly incarcerated individuals experience anxiety, depression, PTSD, and other mental health challenges. Accessing therapy, counseling, and support groups can provide valuable tools for managing these challenges and building resilience. NAMI (National Alliance on Mental Illness) and other mental health organizations offer resources and support

groups for individuals and families affected by mental illness.
Remember, advocacy is a powerful tool. You have the right to advocate for yourself and for other formerly incarcerated individuals. Get involved in local organizations that are working to reform the criminal justice system and promote re-entry success. Share your story and experiences to raise awareness about the challenges and opportunities of re-entry. By advocating for policy changes and challenging stigma, you can help create a more just and equitable society for all.
Finally, remember that re-entry is a journey, not a destination. There will be setbacks and challenges along the way. Don't be afraid to ask for help when you need it. Stay connected to your support network, and celebrate your successes, no matter how small. With perseverance, resilience, and access to the right resources, you can build a fulfilling and productive life after incarceration. I know it isn't easy; however, with help everything it will be. You can do it! I believe in you!

7.3 Advocacy and Empowerment

Re-entering the community isn't simply about finding a place to live or a job; it's about regaining agency and a sense of belonging. It's about shifting from being a system-defined individual to becoming a self-defined community member. This chapter delves into the practical strategies for fostering advocacy and empowerment among individuals transitioning from incarceration, focusing on how we can equip them to navigate the complexities of re-entry with confidence and resilience.
The initial step involves cultivating self-advocacy skills. Many individuals who have been incarcerated have had their decision-making power diminished. Years of institutional living often strip away au-

tonomy, leaving individuals reliant on others for even the simplest choices. Therefore, re-entry programs must prioritize the development of self-advocacy skills, equipping individuals to effectively communicate their needs, assert their rights, and actively participate in decisions that affect their lives. This begins with basic communication skills – learning how to articulate needs clearly and respectfully. Role-playing scenarios can be incredibly valuable here. Simulate interactions with landlords, employers, or social service providers, providing a safe space to practice assertive communication without fear of judgment. Moreover, understanding one's rights is paramount. Legal literacy workshops, tailored to the specific challenges faced by returning citizens, can empower them to navigate the legal landscape with greater confidence. These workshops should cover topics such as employment discrimination, housing rights, and voting rights, equipping individuals to challenge injustices and advocate for their own well-being. Building this skill takes time, consistency, and often, a supportive mentor who can offer guidance and encouragement along the way.

Another crucial aspect of empowerment lies in facilitating access to resources and information. Navigating the myriad of social services, housing options, and employment opportunities can be overwhelming, particularly for those unfamiliar with community resources or lacking the skills to navigate complex bureaucratic systems. Community resource guides, both online and in print, can serve as invaluable tools, providing comprehensive information on local services, eligibility requirements, and contact information. Equally important is the provision of individualized support in accessing these resources. Case managers or peer mentors can assist individuals in completing applications, scheduling appointments, and advocating for their needs within the system. I've seen firsthand how something as simple as help filling out a housing application can be the difference between homelessness and stable living. Beyond tangible resources, access to information is equally critical. Workshops on topics such as financial literacy, parenting skills, and healthy relationships can empower individuals to make informed decisions and build fulfilling lives. It is important to be mindful that it should be adapted to the individual's learning style, and cultural background, increasing the likelihood of engagement and success.

Furthermore, creating opportunities for civic engagement and community involvement is essential. Empowerment is not just about individual self-sufficiency; it's about fostering a sense of belonging and civic responsibility. Encouraging returning citizens to participate in community events, volunteer their time, or join local organizations can help them reconnect with their communities, build social capital, and develop a sense of purpose. Furthermore, involving formerly incarcerated individuals in advocacy efforts related to criminal justice reform can be particularly empowering. Their lived experiences can provide valuable insights into the challenges faced by returning citizens, and their voices can be powerful catalysts for change. I recall one individual, after completing a public speaking course offered through a re-entry program, becoming a vocal advocate for fair housing policies, sharing his own struggles to find stable housing after release. His story resonated deeply with policymakers and community members alike, leading to meaningful policy changes.

Now, let's talk about peer support networks because it represents another potent pathway to empowerment. Connecting individuals with others who have shared similar experiences can foster a sense of camaraderie, reduce feelings of isolation, and provide access to valuable support and guidance. Peer support groups can offer a safe space for individuals to share their struggles, celebrate their successes, and learn from each other's experiences. Moreover, peer mentors can serve as role models, demonstrating that successful re-entry is possible and providing practical advice on navigating the challenges of community life. The key to effective peer support programs is to ensure that they are facilitated by well-trained individuals who can provide guidance, promote positive communication, and maintain confidentiality. It's about creating a community where vulnerability is met with understanding, and challenges are faced together.

In addition to these strategies, promoting educational and vocational opportunities is paramount. Education and employment are key pillars of successful re-entry, providing individuals with the skills, knowledge, and financial resources to build stable and fulfilling lives. Re-entry programs should offer access to educational opportunities ranging from basic literacy classes to college degree programs. Vocational training programs can equip individuals with marketable skills that are in demand in the local job market. Furthermore, providing support with job search skills, such as resume writing, interview preparation, and networking, can increase an individual's chances of securing employment. But it's not just about getting a job, it's about finding meaningful work that aligns with an individual's interests, values, and long-term goals. I've seen many individuals thrive when they are able to pursue careers that tap into their passions and talents.

Finally, it is vital to foster a sense of hope and resilience. Re-entry is a challenging process, and individuals will inevitably face setbacks and obstacles along the way. It is crucial to cultivate a sense of hope and resilience, helping individuals to believe in their ability to overcome challenges and achieve their goals. This can be achieved through positive reinforcement, encouragement, and the celebration of small victories. Additionally, teaching coping skills, such as mindfulness and stress management techniques, can help individuals navigate difficult emotions and maintain a positive outlook. Resilience isn't about avoiding challenges; it's about learning how to bounce back from adversity, stronger and wiser than before.

Ultimately, advocacy and empowerment are not simply programs or services; they are fundamental principles that should guide all aspects of re-entry support. By fostering self-advocacy skills, facilitating access to resources, creating opportunities for civic engagement, promoting peer support networks, and nurturing a sense of hope and resilience, we can empower individuals transitioning from incarceration to become active, engaged, and contributing members of their communities. It requires a commitment to seeing beyond past mistakes and recognizing the potential for positive change within each individual. When we invest in empowerment, we invest in a safer, more just, and more equitable society for all.

www.ingramcontent.com/pod-product-compliance
Lightning Source LLC
LaVergne TN
LVHW022007200926
848481LV00007B/2268